- **BY WHAT FAMOUS NICKNAME ARE THE SPECIAL FORCES MORE COMMONLY KNOWN?**
- **WHO LEAKED THE "PENTAGON PAPERS" TO WHAT REPORTER OF WHAT NEWSPAPER?**
- **WHAT IS A "BOUNCING BETTY"?**
- **CAN YOU NAME THE PREFERRED RIFLE OF THE VC?**

The Vietnam War shaped the lives of an entire generation of Americans. Over fifty-five thousand Americans died there. Yet just a decade after the war's end we are in danger of forgetting what happened in Southeast Asia and at home during those turbulent years.

Now Jeff Stein, former editor of *Veteran,* the monthly magazine of the Vietnam Veterans of America, brings us an important collection of facts. Everything is here—the casualty figures, the history, the heros, and even the movies, from *Coming Home* to *Rambo.*

Here is a book to be used and discussed, to provoke memories and to teach about a time—and a war—that changed our nation.

THE
VIETNAM
FACT
BOOK

Jeff Stein

A DELL BOOK

Published by
Dell Publishing Co., Inc.
1 Dag Hammarskjold Plaza
New York, New York 10017

A small portion of this book first appeared in *Veteran*, April 1985.

Dell ® TM 681510, Dell Publishing Co., Inc.

ISBN: 0-440-19336-2

Printed in the United States of America

October 1987

10 9 8 7 6 5 4 3 2 1

KRI

Contents

FOREWORD   vii

ABOUT THE AUTHOR   ix

1 POLITICS, INTRIGUE, AND DIPLOMACY   1

2 NAMES AND PLACES   20

3 UNITS AND INSIGNIA   47

4 WEAPONS   61

5 THE GROUND WAR   73

6 THE AIR WAR   112

7 THE WAR AT HOME   135

8 VIETNAM IN BOOKS, MOVIES, AND MUSIC   160

FOREWORD

This simple little book was prompted by a poll about Vietnam taken by *The Washington Post* and ABC News in April 1985. Exactly ten years earlier, in the most humiliating military disaster ever suffered by this country, U.S. forces had been evacuated from Saigon in an internationally televised panic.

Yet only a decade after the end of the war, almost half of those polled who were under thirty years old (48 percent) and a third of those over thirty *could not remember which side were we on.* And although almost fifty-five thousand Americans had died in Vietnam over a sixteen-year span, more than half the Americans questioned (57 percent) "did not have a clear idea of what we were fighting for in Vietnam."

At the time of the tenth anniversary of the war's end, fifteen years after my own return from Vietnam, I was the editor and publisher of *Veteran,* the monthly magazine of the Vietnam Veterans of America, Inc. The dismal response to the poll prompted a two-page quiz that appeared in that magazine. That quiz has now grown into *The Vietnam Fact Book.*

It is my hope that high school and college teachers will find this book useful in preparing their students for deeper discussions of the hard questions about Vietnam. This book is not just another question-and-answer book about history. It should lead even the most uninterested reader to a better understanding of key events and personalities of the Vietnam era, as well as the relationship between U.S. domestic politics and conduct of the war.

Vietnam combat veterans and any military buffs, I hope, will be challenged by the separate chapters on weapons, units and insignia, and the air and ground wars. More for the general reader (and untold numbers of aging war protesters), I've also included chapters on the war at home and Vietnam in music, books, and movies.

Although a score of books and documents were consulted in the preparation of this book, some proved particularly useful. First among these were: *The Vietnam War Almanac*, by Colonel Harry G. Summers, Jr. (Facts on File, 1985), a most valuable glossary of names, places, military units, and terms; *An International History of the Vietnam War*, Volumes 1 and 2, by R. B. Smith (St. Martin's Press, 1983–86); *The Rise and Fall of an American Army: U.S. Ground Forces in Vietnam, 1965–1973*, by Shelby L. Stanton (Presidio, 1985); *Vietnam Voices: Perspectives on the War Years*, by John Clark Pratt (Viking, 1984); and the Time-Life/Boston Publishing Company series, *The Vietnam Experience*. A very helpful source for the chapter on the war at home was *Who Spoke Up?* by Nancy Zaroulis and Gerald Sullivan (Doubleday, 1984).

Special thanks go to the Vietnam Veterans of America, Inc. (2001 S Street N.W., Washington, DC 20009), which permitted me the pleasure of editing and publishing its magazine for a year—especially Robert Muller, president, John Terzano, vice president, and David Addlestone, counsel. For iced tea and sympathy in the last, breakneck hours of putting this book together, Gigi Wizowaty and Janna Murphy have our warmest gratitude. Finally, none of this would have happened without the kind assistance of my agent, Gail Ross.

—Jeff Stein
Washington, D.C.
August 1986

About the Author

Jeff Stein served as a U.S. Army Intelligence case officer in South Vietnam in 1968–69. He holds an M.A. in Asian Studies from the University of California, Berkeley. Presently he is a foreign news editor with UPI in Washington, D.C.

Marc Leepson, who provided invaluable research, is a former staff writer with *Congressional Quarterly*'s Editorial Research Reports. He served with the U.S. Army's First Logistical Command in Qui Nhon, Vietnam, in 1967–68. He is books editor and a columnist for the VVA's *Veteran*.

1

POLITICS, INTRIGUE, AND DIPLOMACY

1 Who wrote *The Quiet American,* and on the life of what real-life American intelligence official was it based?

ANS: Graham Greene was the author. CIA agent Edward G. Lansdale, sent to Saigon to rally the South Vietnamese government against the Communists, was said to be Greene's model.

2 To what did "third force" refer?

ANS: A non-Communist acceptable both to the Saigon military establishment and to the Communists. It was a term used by Americans who sought a political alternative to the continuing war, which they reckoned could be lost without a "third force."

3 What decision regarding Indochina was made at the Yalta conference of allies near the end of World War II?

ANS: Indochina would be made a French "trusteeship," which meant that Paris would reestablish its colonial rule.

4 Which bureau of the U.S. State Department—European or Asian—favored returning Vietnam to French control?

ANS: European.

5 At the time of the Japanese surrender in August 1945, who controlled Hanoi?
  a) Vichy France
  b) Japan
  c) China
  d) Britain

ANS: b.

6 Who controlled Saigon then?
  a) Vichy France
  b) Japan
  c) China
  d) Britain

ANS: d. On the day Japan surrendered, the Allies ordered Britain to take control of Saigon. It did—with Japanese help.

7 What Vietnamese group led by Ho Chi Minh helped rescue downed U.S. pilots in Vietnam during World War II?

ANS: the Viet Minh.

8 What does *Viet Minh* mean?

ANS: *Viet Minh* is the short form of *Viet Nam Dong Minh Hoi,* or "Vietnamese Independence League."

9 True or false: The main supporter and financial backer of the Viet Minh in 1945 was the United States.

ANS: True.

10 Why did the United States support the Viet Minh?

ANS: Because it was a coalition of Communist and nationalist groups that had helped the United States during the war, and it had no competition for political power in Annam.

11 When did the Viet Minh, under Ho Chi Minh, take control of Hanoi?

ANS: On September 2, 1945.

12 Did France start fighting the Viet Minh then?

ANS: No. France agreed to recognize Viet Minh control of North Vietnam and to hold elections in the south, with the goal of reunifying the nation, within five years.

13 Did the United States have a military representative in Saigon in September 1945?

ANS: Yes, an OSS team.

14 Why?

ANS: To oversee the orderly transfer of power in South Vietnam back to France, as agreed at Yalta.

15 When did the elections to reunify Vietnam take place?

ANS: They didn't. The French refused to honor the terms they had negotiated with the Viet Minh in 1945.

16 True or false: In 1946, the French established the Republic of Cochinchina to deny the Communists power in the south.

ANS: True.

17 Who was made the leader of this new Vietnam by the French?
  a) Bao Don
  b) Bao Chi
  c) Bao Oau
  d) Bao Dai
  e) Dai Uy

ANS: d.

18 What was his title?
  a) premier
  b) prime minister
  c) emperor
  d) president
  e) regent

ANS: c.

19 Did the United States throw its support behind Bao Dai?

ANS: No. It quickly began to look for a more "democratic" substitute.

20 When did armed hostilities between Ho Chi Minh's Viet Minh and the French resume?

ANS: In December 1946.

21 The United States had backed Ho Chi Minh earlier. Did it continue its support now?

ANS: No.

22 Which two of the following countries gave official recognition to Ho's Democratic Republic of Vietnam in January 1950?
   a) France
   b) Soviet Union
   c) China
   d) United States

ANS: b and c.

23 True or false: In 1950, the United States began to provide military aid to France in its struggle against Ho Chi Minh.

ANS: True.

24 True or false: That year the United States provided 10 percent of France's war budget in Indochina.

ANS: False. It was 40 percent.

25 True or False: By 1954 the United States had withdrawn its support for the French.

ANS: False. The United States was providing $1 billion for its Indochina campaign.

26 By then, Ngo Dinh Diem was
   a) president of North Vietnam
   b) president of South Vietnam
   c) leader of Viet Cong

d) living in the United States
e) prime minister under Bao Dai

ANS: e.

27 A peace conference began in what city to settle the war?

ANS: Geneva, Switzerland.

Match these names with the governments they represented at Geneva:

28 Mendes-France	a)	United States
29 Pham Van Dong	b)	Russia
30 Andrei Gromyko	c)	Britain
31 Anthony Eden	d)	France
32 John Foster Dulles	e)	Hanoi
33 Chou En-lai	f)	China

ANS: 28-d, 29-e, 30-b, 31-c, 32-a, 33-f.

34 Who didn't sign the Geneva protocol on Indochina?

ANS: The United States, South Vietnam (which was not represented, in any case), and China.

35 One of the agreements at Geneva was to divide Vietnam in half. Where?

ANS: At the 17th parallel.

36 Another agreement was to hold an election in July 1956. Who won?

ANS: Nobody; once again, the election was never held.

37 How did Ngo Dinh Diem come into power in Saigon?
a) national referendum organized by the United States
b) military coup
c) flown in by the CIA
d) backroom deal with the Viet Minh
e) free and fair elections

ANS: a.

38 What did the referendum offer?

ANS: A choice between monarchy under Bao Dai or a republic with Diem as president.

39 Of the 6 million votes cast, Diem won by what percentage?
a) 51
b) 66
c) 77
d) 87
e) 98.6

ANS: e.

40 When Diem proclaimed the Republic of Vietnam in 1955, who were his principal backers?
a) French socialists
b) Cardinal Spellman and CIA
c) the Kennedys
d) the U.S. State Department
e) Senator Mike Mansfield
f) Vice President Nixon

ANS: everybody but a.

41 The majority religion in South Vietnam is

ANS: Buddhism.

42 Ngo Dinh Diem's brother was the head of the hated secret police. What was his name?

ANS: Ngo Dinh Nhu.

43 What happened to Ngo Dinh Diem and his brother on November 2, 1963?
a) They were forced into exile.
b) They were shot by Communists.
c) They were overthrown and murdered by United States–backed Saigon generals.

ANS: c.

44 Who was the U.S. ambassador to Vietnam at the time when Diem was overthrown?
a) Henry Luce
b) Henry Cabot Lodge
c) William Whitehead

ANS: b.

45 His nickname was "Black Luigi," and he played a key role in the Diem overthrow. Who was he?

ANS: Lucien Conein, a U.S. Army major and CIA agent. He was the go-between with the generals who overthrew Diem.

46 True or false: Diem and President Kennedy were assassinated within weeks of each other.

ANS: True.

FACT _____

Madame Nhu, the sister-in-law of Ngo Dinh Diem, had been traveling in the United States for several weeks prior to President Kennedy's assassination, holding press conferences and telling anyone who would listen that the White House was plotting her brother-in-law's ouster. Her frenetic, heavily accented accusations in that age of relative political innocence found no audience. Leaving the United States shortly following Diem's assassination, she hysterically claimed that JFK would be next. She eventually settled into a quiet exile in Rome.

_____

47 What was the name of the armed Vietnamese gangs that controlled Saigon's drug, prostitution, and gambling rackets?
a) Cao Dai
b) Hoa Hao
c) Binh Xuyen

ANS: c.

48 Why were the Binh Xuyen powerful?

ANS: Because they were led by Bay Vien, Saigon's version of Al Capone, and backed by the French secret police, they were crushed by Diem in 1954.

49 True or false: Two young generals, Nguyen Van Thieu and Nguyen Cao Ky, formed a coalition government following Diem's assassination.

ANS: False.

50 In June 1964, President Lyndon Johnson chose Blair Seaborn to secretly sound out Hanoi on its willingness to negotiate a way out of the war. Who was Seaborn?

ANS: Seaborn was a Canadian diplomat and delegate to the three-member International Control Commission, which was charged with overseeing the Geneva accords.

51 What did Johnson promise about Vietnam during his campaign against Goldwater in 1964?
    a) "to seek no wider war"
    b) "to seek a military solution"
    c) "to seek peace"
    d) "to go to Korea"

ANS: a.

52 Which was the reason most likely for North Vietnam's Pham Van Dong's turning down LBJ's 1965 peace overture?
    a) Saigon was winning on the battlefield.
    b) Hanoi was winning on the battlefield.
    c) Hanoi wanted U.S. troops in South Vietnam.

ANS: b.

53 In September 1964, what Secretary-General of the United Nations became involved in trying to start direct negotiations between the United States and Hanoi?

ANS: U Thant.

54 In 1965, Marshal Josep Broz Tito of Yugoslavia hosted a conference of seventeen nonaligned nations. Their leaders urged "the parties concerned to start . . . negotiations without . . . preconditions." LBJ rejected this urging because
    a) he didn't want to negotiate.
    b) he had "preconditions."
    c) the phrase "parties concerned" implied that the Viet Cong were an independent unit.

ANS: c.

55 In a famous speech at Johns Hopkins University in 1965, LBJ proposed to spend how much money in Southeast Asia once the war ended?
a) $100 million
b) $500 million
c) $1 billion

ANS: c.

56 When did LBJ order the first bombing halt over North Vietnam?

ANS: May 13, 1965.

57 What did some Buddhists do that forced a major political crisis for the United States in 1966?

ANS: They burned themselves to death in the streets.

58 Under whom did Nguyen Cao Ky serve as air force chief?

ANS: Nguyen Khanh.

59 Who was Nguyen Khanh?

ANS: A military hack who ruled briefly after Diem.

60 True or false: During his rule Khanh called for an invasion of North Vietnam.

ANS: True.

61 Who was the dashing former pilot, Khanh's air force chief, later to be premier?
   a) Big Minh
   b) Little Minh
   c) William Westmoreland
   d) Nguyen Cao Ky
   e) Pham Van Dong
   f) Le Duc Tho

ANS: d.

62 What Saigon politician, who eventually became vice president of South Vietnam, caused an uproar when he said he "admired" Hitler?

ANS: Nguyen Cao Ky.

63 Who was elected president of South Vietnam in 1967?
   a) Nguyen Van Thieu
   b) Nguyen Cao Ky
   c) Duong van Minh

ANS: a.

64 Who did Thieu appoint as his prime minister?

ANS: Nguyen Cao Ky.

65 What former Air Vietnam stewardess and Saigon politician's wife had her eyes surgically Westernized?

ANS: Mai, the wife of Nguyen Cao Ky.

66 True or false: On February 8, 1967, LBJ sent a secret letter to Ho Chi Minh asking for "direct talks" leading to peace.

ANS: True.

67 True or false: Ho Chi Minh agreed to talks if the United States stopped bombing.

ANS: True.

68 On March 21, 1967, what did Ho Chi Minh do with LBJ's letter?

ANS: He made it public.

69 What was "McNamara's defection"?

ANS: The defense secretary, Robert S. McNamara, concluded in 1967 that the United States could not win the war.

70 When did McNamara leave office?

ANS: On February 29, 1968.

71 On June 17, 1967, McNamara formed a secret Pentagon task force to write an internal history of the Vietnam War. What was this report eventually called?

ANS: The Pentagon Papers.

72 What was the name of the ultraright Vietnamese political party that was opposed to Thieu and other United States–backed Saigon leaders?

ANS: The Viet Nam Quoc Dan Dang, or Vietnamese Nationalist Party, known by its initials, VNQDD.

73 When did Henry Kissinger first become involved in secret diplomacy regarding Vietnam?

ANS: In 1967, Kissinger, a political adviser to Nelson Rockefeller and secretly advising Hubert Humphrey's burgeoning presidential campaign as well, approached two Frenchmen with ties to Ho Chi Minh and engaged them to carry messages from LBJ to Hanoi.

74 One of the two Frenchmen whom Kissinger approached was M. Aubrac. What was Aubrac's special relationship with Ho Chi Minh?

ANS: Ho had become the godfather of Aubrac's son in 1946, when he had stayed in Paris during postwar peace talks.

75 On September 3, 1967, with a combined total of what percent of the vote did Thieu and Ky declare themselves reelected president and vice president of South Vietnam?
a) 35
b) 45
c) 55
d) 65
e) 95

ANS: a.

76 What was the name of intense political turmoil that China was going through at this time?

ANS: The Great Proletarian Cultural Revolution—cultural revolution, for short.

77 What was China's advice to Hanoi at this time?

ANS: Draw the United States into a protracted land war on the Asian mainland.

78 In December 1967, what glamorous American woman visited Phnom Penh at Prince Sihanouk's invitation with all the trappings of a head of state?

ANS: Jacqueline Kennedy.

79 In January 1968, a U.S. mission headed by Chester Bowles arrived in Phnom Penh. Sihanouk was reported to have said that he would not be opposed to what, of Vietcong troops in Cambodia?

ANS: "Hot pursuit."

80 Meanwhile, back in Saigon in the last week of January, what major military event was secretly taking shape?

ANS: The Tet Offensive.

81 On March 12, 1968, what Democratic U.S. senator made a surprisingly strong showing against LBJ, in the New Hampshire primary?

ANS: Eugene McCarthy.

82 Four days later, another Democratic senator, this one from New York, entered the campaign for President. Who was he?

ANS: Robert F. Kennedy.

83   When LBJ announced on March 31, 1968, that he wouldn't run for reelection, he also announced a bombing halt, to go into effect where?
   a) above the 17th parallel
   b) above the 20th parallel
   c) all over North Vietnam

ANS: b.

84   Where and when was Dr. Martin Luther King, Jr., murdered?

ANS: In Memphis, Tennessee, on April 4, 1968.

85   Who was arrested and charged with the murder?

ANS: James Earl Ray, Jr.

86   On May 3, 1968, Washington and Hanoi announced the biggest diplomatic breakthrough of the war from secret talks. What was it?

ANS: They would start negotiations in Paris the following week to end the war.

87   When and where was Robert F. Kennedy murdered?

ANS: June 6, 1968, in Los Angeles.

88   Who was arrested and charged with the murder?

ANS: Sirhan Sirhan.

89　True or false: Both Sirhan Sirhan and James Earl Ray said they had carried out their assassinations in support of the Vietnam War.

ANS: False.

90　Meanwhile, what extraordinary military event occurred in Europe on August 20, 1968?

ANS: The Russian invasion of Czechoslovakia.

91　Who were the Democratic presidential and vice-presidential candidates nominated on August 29, 1968?

ANS: Hubert Humphrey and Edmund Muskie.

92　What would be the only accomplishment of the Paris peace negotiators in the following six months?

ANS: Determining the shape of the table.

93　What shape was that?

ANS: Round.

94　What Communist precondition for negotiations did LBJ finally agree to, and when?

ANS: An end to all U.S. bombing of North Vietnam, on November 1, 1968.

95　Was there any political significance to that date?

ANS: Yes. It was four days before the U.S. presidential elections.

96 What kind of plan to end the war did Richard Nixon claim he had developed during the campaign?

ANS: A "secret" plan.

97 Who were elected U.S. President and Vice President on November 5, 1968?

ANS: Richard M. Nixon and Spiro T. Agnew.

98 True or false: Henry Kissinger became the new U.S. secretary of state.

ANS: False. It was William A. Rogers.

99 Who was the new secretary of defense?

ANS: Melvin Laird.

100 Who replaced Walt Rostow as national security adviser?

ANS: Henry A. Kissinger.

101 When and through what major foreign ambassador to the United States did Nixon and Kissinger first launch their secret pursuit of a peace settlement?

ANS: In March 1969, Kissinger asked the Soviet ambassador to the United States, Anatoly Dobrynin, to act as a go-between. Nothing came of the effort.

102 When did Kissinger make his first secret and personal contact with Hanoi to negotiate an end to the war?

ANS: In August 1969.

103 In these secret talks who was Hanoi's first representative?

ANS: Xuan Thuy.

2

NAMES AND PLACES

1 The capital of North Vietnam was————.

ANS: Hanoi.

2 The capital of South Vietnam was————.

ANS: Saigon.

3 What is the capital of Vietnam today?

ANS: Hanoi.

4 What was Saigon renamed at the end of the war?

ANS: Ho Chi Minh City.

5 Who was Nguyen Ai Quoc?
  a) Nguyen Van Thieu
  b) Nguyen Huu Tho
  c) Ho Chi Minh

ANS: c. It was Ho's Communist code name, which meant "Nguyen the Patriot" (literally, he "who loves his country").

6 What is the name of the river separating North and South Vietnam?
   a) Hai Phong
   b) Ben Hai
   c) Perfume River

ANS: b.

7 Where is the Red River?

ANS: In North Vietnam.

8 In the early 1960s, the U.S. Embassy singled out what skeptical *New York Times* reporter in Saigon as being the major problem for the United States in winning the war?

ANS: Homer Bigart.

9 Identify the speaker and circumstances of this famous quote: "Another westerner come to lose his reputation to Ho chi Minh."

ANS: *New York Times* reporter Homer Bigart, describing the arrival in 1961 of Henry Cabot Lodge, the latest U.S. ambassador to South Vietnam.

10 Who was the author of *The Best and the Brightest*, a profile of key U.S. civilian and military leaders during the Vietnam War?

ANS: David Halberstam.

11 Who commanded the troops that entered My Lai-4 on March 16, 1968, and massacred hundreds of Vietnamese civilians?

ANS: Lt. William Calley.

12 What U.S. Army unit was he from?

ANS: The Americal Division.

13 Because of the number of Vietcong in the area, U.S. troops had nicknamed it
  a) Redtown
  b) Gook City
  c) Pinkville

ANS: Pinkville.

14 But it was also known as
  a) My Tho
  b) Son Tay
  c) Son My

ANS: c.

15 What reporter who uncovered the massacre and won a Pulitzer Prize for it?

ANS: Seymour Hersh.

16 What U.S. Army general headed the investigative inquiry into the My Lai events?
  a) Creighton Abrams
  b) William Peers
  c) William Westmoreland

ANS: b.

17 Who was Lt. Gen. Samuel B. Koster?

ANS: The commanding officer of the Americal Division. He was eventually convicted of wrongful conduct and of cover-up of the My Lai massacre.

FACT

Although Seymour Hersh went on to earn great fame as a *New York Times* reporter and authored several more books, he was still a freelance writer in November 1969, when he read a brief wire service report about the court martial of Calley for needless civilian deaths under his command a year and a half earlier.

Hersh, his curiosity piqued, obtained a small grant from the Fund for Investigative Journalism. It paid his air fare to an Army base in Georgia, where he found Calley. Hersh persuaded him to tell the whole story of what happened in My Lai.

Hersh did not write his scoop for *The New York Times*. It was distributed by the small alternative Dispatch News Service to about fifty newspapers, most of which bought it sight unseen from its chief, David Obst, now a Hollywood book and movie agent. Hersh went on to write two books about the affair, *My Lai 4: A Report on the Massacre and Its Aftermath* (Random House, 1970), which won a Pulitzer Prize, and *Cover Up* (Random House, 1972), which described another massacre in My Lai the same day, the CIA's role in it, and the conspiracy at the highest military levels to withold the truth about it from the public.

18 Who was Lt. William Calley's superior at My Lai?

ANS: Captain Ernest Medina.

19 What Army photographer took the pictures of the massacre that were later published to great public horror in *Life* magazine?
a) David Hume Kennerly
b) Robert Capa
c) Ronald Haeberle

ANS: c.

20 What was the name of the village of which it was said that we had to destroy it in order to save it?

ANS: Ben Tre.

The CIA made use of several ethnic minority groups during the war. Match the common names of these groups with their identities.

21	Montangards	a)	Chinese-Vietnamese
22	Meo	b)	Laotian tribesmen
23	Nung	c)	Central Highlanders
24	Khmer Serai	d)	Cambodians

ANS: 21-c, 22-b, 23-a, 24-d.

25 *Montagnard* is a French term that means what?

ANS: Mountain people.

26 What was the Americans' diminutive name for them?

ANS: "Yards."

27 What derogatory term did the Vietnamese use for them?

ANS: Moi, or Meo, which could also mean "SAVAGE" and was often applied to diverse tribes of indigenous hill people.

FACT

Like the American Indians, there are many so-called Montagnard tribes: Hre, Chan, Tuong, Mien, Jarai, Bahnar, Mnong, Sedang, Halang, Ragulai, Rongao, Bong, Nongao, Koho, Ma, Chil, Drung.

28 What U.S. Army unit made special use of the Yards?

ANS: The Green Berets, or Special Forces.

29 The Parrot's Beak is an area
  a) in southern Laos
  b) on the North Vietnam–China border
  c) part of Cambodia penetrating South Vietnam

ANS: c.

30 Where are the islands Hon Ngu and Hon Me?

ANS: In the Tonkin Gulf.

31 What was Operation Ranch Hand?
  a) a U.S. Food for Peace program
  b) an effort to bring cattle to Vietnam
  c) U.S. aerial herbicide spraying

ANS: c.

32 What did U.S. C-131s spray over Vietnam?
  a) Agent Orange

    b) Agent Blue
    c) Agent White

ANS: a, b, and c. All three were used for deforestation and crop destruction.

33 What was MACV?

ANS: Military Assistance Command, Vietnam—the central command for U.S. forces in Vietnam.

34 What was MACV's nickname?

ANS: Pentagon East.

35 What was the USARV?

ANS: U.S. Army, Vietnam.

36 What was Tan Son Nhut?

ANS: The major air base and commercial airport in South Vietnam, located in suburban Saigon.

37 True or false: The last two U.S. servicemen killed in action in Vietnam were two U.S. Marine security guards who were hit by shrapnel at the U.S. Embassy on April 28, 1975.

ANS: False. They were hit at Tan Son Nhut.

38 What was Cho Lon?

ANS: The Chinese section of Saigon.

39 What Saigon police general shot a captured Vietcong in the head during the Tet Offensive—an act which was forever memorialized on film?

ANS: Gen. Nguyen Ngoc Loan.

40 What sparsely inhabited area on Vietnam's central coast was turned into a major U.S. base during the war?
  a) Lai Day
  b) Phu Bai
  c) Chao Ong
  d) Dien Cai Dao
  e) Chu Lai

ANS: e.

41 The French called it Cap St. Jacques. It became a major in-country, south coastal R&R spot for GIs during the war?

ANS: Vung Tau.

42 What major street in Saigon turned into a honky-tonk strip during the war?

ANS: Tu Do Street.

43 What was the major Vietcong base area south of Saigon in the Delta?

ANS: Plain of Reeds.

44 Which of the following was *not* among the five provinces of French Indochina?
  a) Annam
  b) Cambodia

   c) Cochinchina
   d) Laos
   e) Thailand
   f) Tonkin

ANS: e.

45 The major CIA-owned airline in Southeast Asia during the war was

ANS: Air America.

46 This was a jungle fortress of Communist troops in the *south* throughout the war:
   a) Red River Valley
   b) Ashau Valley
   c) Valley of the Dolls
   d) Anh Com Valley

ANS: b.

47 Who succeeded Gen. William Westmoreland as commander of U.S. forces in Vietnam?

ANS: Gen. Creighton Abrams.

48 What CIA officer went public during the war to challenge official U.S. estimates of Communist troop strength?
   a) William Colby
   b) Victor Marchetti
   c) Samuel Adams
   d) George Ball
   e) Frank Snepp

ANS: c.

49 Victor Marchetti wrote a famous exposé about secret U.S. government operations. He had been
a) a U.S. Army general
b) a CIA officer
c) the Italian ambassador to North Vietnam

ANS: b.

50 Who was William Colby?

ANS: CIA station chief in Saigon who later became CIA director.

51 Who was George Ball?

ANS: A State Department "dove" in the Kennedy Administration who argued against sending troops to Vietnam.

52 Who was Frank Snepp?

ANS: A former CIA analyst who wrote a critical book about the Vietnam pullout called *Decent Interval.*

53 What was the significance of Snepp's book?
a) Its publication was suppressed by the CIA.
b) He disappeared after it was published.
c) The Supreme Court ruled he couldn't keep royalties from it because he violated his secrecy oath.

ANS: c.

54 True or false: The Iron Triangle was the area where Laos, North Vietnam, and South Vietnam converged on the Ho Chi Minh Trail.

ANS: False. It was a Communist stronghold in the Delta.

55 True or false: Da Nang is the capital of the Central Highlands.

ANS: False. It is on the coast of South Vietnam, 380 miles north of Saigon.

56 Where and when did the first U.S. Marine combat units arrive in South Vietnam?

ANS: On Nam O, or Red Beach, just north of Da Nang, on March 8, 1965.

57 What was their original unit designation?

ANS: The Marine Expeditionary Force. It was quickly renamed the Third Marine Amphibious Force because the former sounded too French.

58 Who was Patrick Nugent, and why was his presence in South Vietnam so noteworthy?

ANS: Nugent was the husband of LBJ's daughter Lucy; he was assigned to Operation Ranch Hand.

59 What other LBJ in-law served in South Vietnam?

ANS: U.S. Marine Captain Charles Robb.

60 Who was Paul Harkins?

ANS: A U.S. Army general and chief of the U.S. military mission in Saigon during the Kennedy Administration.

61 A place called Nui Ba Dinh fascinated and irritated U.S. commanders throughout the long war. What was it?

ANS: A mountaintop rising out of the flat delta south of Saigon. It was controlled by the Vietcong throughout the war.

62 His biographer called him "the inevitable general." AP correspondent Peter Arnett said he wanted to be "CINC world." Who was it?

ANS: Gen. William Westmoreland.

63 True or false: LBJ sent Westmoreland to Vietnam as chief of U.S. forces.

ANS: False. Kennedy sent him.

64 At the time, Kennedy's ambassador was:
  a) Paul Harkin
  b) Henry Cabot Lodge
  c) McGeorge Bundy

ANS: b.

65 What was a Starlight Scope?

ANS: A scope attached to rifles that aided night vision.

66 What did RMK-BRJ refer to?

ANS: Raymond, Morris, Knudson–Brown, Root, Jones. It was the huge consortium that was in charge of construction in South Vietnam.

67   Who was the last emperor of Vietnam?

ANS: Bao Dai.

68   Which town in the Central Highlands was the first target of the final North Vietnamese offensive in 1975?
a) Ban Me Thuot
b) DaLat
c) Pleiku

ANS: a.

69   What two brothers were among the architects of Vietnam War policy in their roles as advisers to Presidents Kennedy and Johnson?

ANS: The Bundy brothers, McGeorge and William.

70   Who served as U.S. ambassador to Saigon from April 1967 to March 1973?
a) William Bundy
b) Paul Harkin
c) Maxwell Taylor
d) Henry Cabot Lodge
e) Ellsworth Bunker

ANS: e.

71   What was the Battle of Bunker's Bunker?

ANS: The Vietcong invasion of the Embassy grounds during Tet in 1968.

72   Who was "Lightning Joe" Collins?

ANS: An Air Force general who served in World War I, World War II, and Korea. He was sent to South Vietnam by Ike in 1954 to organize agrarian reform and military training programs. When Diem balked, Collins advised Ike against aiding him.

73   What was a "gook"?

ANS: In GI derogatory slang, any Vietnamese person.

74   What was CORDS?

ANS: Civil Operations and Revolutionary Development Support, also known as the "pacification" program.

75   What was a "strategic hamlet"?

ANS: A small village created to house Vietnamese peasants and isolate them from the rural Vietcong.

76   The Communist nerve center was sought by U.S. troops throughout the long war but never found. Its acronym was COSVN. What did it stand for?

ANS: Central Office for South Vietnam.

77   Who was Robert E. Cushman?

ANS: A Marine Corps general who headed I Corps. Later he was deputy director of the CIA.

78   What and where was Dalat?

ANS: A resort area in the Central Highlands favored by the Saigon elite.

79 What was a GI's favorite acronym in Vietnam?
   a) MACV
   b) USARV
   c) C-SPAN
   d) DMZ
   e) DEROS

ANS: e. DEROS stood for "date eligible to return from overseas."

80 Who was known as the Dragon Lady?

ANS: Madame Ngo Dinh Nhu, Ngo Dinh Diem's powerful sister-in-law.

81 How did Madame Nhu notoriously characterize the self-immolation of Buddhist monks protesting her brother-in-law's policies in 1962–63?
   a) "chicken pot pies"
   b) "barbecues"
   c) "hamburger hills"
   d) "sweet and sour"

ANS: b.

82 Where was "hell in a very small place"?

ANS: Dienbienphu, so characterized by French author Bernard Fall.

83 What was the K-9 Corps?

ANS: German shepherds used by U.S. troops for sentry and surveillance.

84   Describe the flag of the Republic of Vietnam.

ANS: Horizontal red bars on a yellow field.

85   What is a "dust-off"?

ANS: A medivac helicopter.

86   In intelligence work, what does a case officer do?

ANS: He or she controls local spies.

87   EOD teams had some of the most dangerous duty in Vietnam. What did they do?

ANS: The Explosive Ordnance Disposal teams defused mines, booby traps, and satchel charges.

88   They flew in little Cessnas above battle areas, well within range of enemy guns, directing the sorties of powerful U.S. jets flying overhead. What were they called?
   a) FACs
   b) DACs
   c) MAX
   d) PACKs
   e) RACKs

ANS: a. FACs were forward air controllers.

89   What does *Vietcong* mean?

ANS: It's short for "Vietnamese Communist" (Vietcong San).

90   When did the National Liberation Front make its public debut?
   a) 1954
   b) 1960
   c) 1963
   d) 1969

ANS: b, on December 20.

91   What was the name Prince Sihanouk gave to the Cambodian Communists?

ANS: Khmer Rouge.

92   Who were the Khmer Serai?

ANS: Anti-Communist Cambodians living in Vietnam organized by the CIA.

93   What was the Communist PRG?

ANS: The Provisional Revolutionary Government of South Vietnam, i.e., the Vietcong. It was created in 1968 as a successor to the NLF.

94   In the PRG, who was Madame Nguyen Thi Binh?

ANS: She was the PRG's foreign minister and its representative at the Paris peace talks in the early 1970s.

95   What senator, the powerful chairman of the Senate Foreign Relations Committee, held critical hearings on Vietnam in February 1966?

ANS: J. William Fulbright of Arkansas.

96 The CBS television network was heavily scored for not broadcasting the Fulbright hearings. What—notoriously—did it run instead?

ANS: Reruns of *I Love Lucy.*

97 True or false: A tunnel rat was a Vietcong who lived underground throughout the entire war.

ANS: False. It was a U.S. GI who searched for the Vietcong in their tunnels.

98 During the war Cu Chi was
  a) a Brazilian dancer
  b) headquarters of the Twenty-fifth Infantry Division
  c) the most extensive maze of Vietcong tunnels
  d) body lice
  e) a tropical bird indigenous to the Parrot's Beak

ANS: b and c.

99 Was Marble Mountain near Hue, Da Nang, or Chu Lai?

ANS: Da Nang.

100 A ——— base was at the foot of Marble Mountain; a ——— hospital was inside it.

ANS: U.S.; Vietcong.

101 Who was Vo Nguyen Giap?

ANS: The minister of defense of North Vietnam until 1975. Giap was the architect of Communist military strategy until 1975, when he was replaced by his protégé, Gen. Van Tien Dung.

Identify the following:
102 U Dorn
103 U Minh
104 U Tapao
105 U Thant

ANS: 102: a U.S. air base in Thailand. 103: a managrove swamp along Vietnam's southern coast, which was a Vietcong base area; 104: a U.S. air base in Thailand; 105: a Burmese leader who became Secretary General of the United Nations.

106 In Vietnamese, *xin loi* (pronounced "sin loy") means what?

ANS: "So sorry" or "excuse me." In GI slang, "sorry about that."

107 In GI slang, what did "lifer" mean?

ANS: It was a derogatory term used by GIs for career military men.

108 In GI slang, "number one" meant ———; "number ten" meant ———.

ANS: great; awful.

109 Who was Le Duc Tho, and what does he have in common with Henry Kissinger?

ANS: Tho, Hanoi's principal negotiator, won the Nobel Peace with Henry Kissinger in 1973.

Are the following true or false?
110 Bangkok is west of Saigon
111 Hanoi is east of Phnom Penh
112 Souvanna Phouma is north of Saigon
113 Da Nang is south of Cam Ranh Bay

ANS: 110 and 111 are true; 112 and 113 are false.

114 True or false: Both Vietnam and Laos now maintain full diplomatic relations with the United States.

ANS: False. The United States has no relations with Hanoi, and Laos–United States relations are on the chargé d'affaires level.

115 Where is the Perfume River—near Da Nang, Saigon, or Hue?

ANS: Near Hue.

116 Who was the last president of South Vietnam?

ANS: Nguyen Van "Big" Minh.

Where did the following Saigon politicians flee at the end of the war:
117 Nguyen Van Thieu
118 Nguyen Cao Ky
119 Gen. Nguyen Ngoc Loan

ANS: 117: To Taiwan, then London; 118: To Virginia, then California, where he owned a liquor store; 119: To Arlington, Virginia, where he owns a restaurant.

120   Did troops from Taiwan ever fight in Vietnam?

ANS: No. In October 1964, the Republic of China furnished an advisory team of twenty to thirty political warfare and medical specialists to Saigon. Taiwan also provided substantial economic and technical assistance.

121   What was a Spooky?

ANS: An AC-47 fixed-wing gunship.

122   The middle name of LBJ adviser Walt Rostow was the same as the last name of what famous nineteenth-century poet?
   a) Dickinson
   b) Whitman
   c) Hawthorne
   d) Poe

ANS: b.

123   True or false: Dr. Tom Dooley, who provided years of medical service to rural Laotians, returned from Indochina in 1965 and denounced the U.S. war effort.

ANS: False. Dooley always supported the war.

124   Did Gen. George Patton head a tank unit in Vietnam?

ANS: No. Col. George S. Patton, son of the famed World War II tank commander, headed the Eleventh Armored Cavalry in Vietnam.

125   What did Michelin have to do with Vietnam?

ANS: Throughout the war it operated a large rubber plantation that often was home to division-size Communist units.

126 **How often did the Vietnamese Tet holiday occur during the war?**

ANS: Every year, from late January to early February.

127 **In what year did the famous Tet Offensive take place?**

ANS: 1968.

128 **Who were Bloods?**

ANS: The term black soldiers often used to refer to themselves.

129 **Who was Daniel "Chappie" James, and why should we remember his name in connection with Vietnam?**

ANS: Air Force General James was the highest-ranking black officer in the service and in Vietnam.

130 **True or false: Thomas Moorer was the admiral who, as chairman of the Joint Chiefs of Staff, oversaw "Vietnamization."**

ANS: True.

131 **What is the significance of the names Gruening and Morse?**

ANS: They were the only two senators to vote against the Gulf of Tonkin resolution.

132 Who was Fritz Nolting?
   a) San Francisco Giants star outfielder drafted to Vietnam
   b) senator from Minnesota who opposed the war
   c) senator from South Carolina who favored the war
   d) U.S. ambassador to Vietnam from 1961 to 1963
   e) head of MACV in 1965–67

ANS: d.

133 True or false: Daniel Ellsberg served as a U.S. Marine officer in Vietnam.

ANS: True.

134 Tony Russo is associated with Ellsberg in the history of the war. Why?

ANS: Russo, who headed the RAND corporation's program of interviewing former Vietcong, met Ellsberg in Saigon and later stood trial for helping him steal the Pentagon Papers.

135 How many POWs came home from Hanoi in March 1973?
   a) 255
   b) 315
   c) 496
   d) 590
   e) 717

ANS: d.

136 What were PSYOPs?
   a) intelligence operations
   b) propaganda teams
   c) hit teams (named after the Greek monster)
   d) psychological warfare operations.

ANS: d.

137 What was Rung Sat?

ANS: The swampy section of the Saigon and Dong Nai rivers, in which Vietcong units hid water mines aimed at South Vietnamese ships.

138 What former Rhodes scholar from Georgia, a World War II Army infantry officer, became secretary of state in the Kennedy Administration and played an active role in determining U.S. military policy in Vietnam?

ANS: Dean Rusk.

139 Who was Chris Noel?

ANS: A female disc jockey on Armed Forces Radio.

140 What were Ruff-Puffs?

ANS: Local Vietnamese militia groups (RFPF: Regional and Popular Forces).

141 What did SEALORDS refer to?

ANS: The name is an acronym for Southeast Asia Lake, Ocean, River, and Delta Strategy. It was a joint U.S. Navy–South Vietnamese Navy operation patrolling rivers in South Vietnam.

142 Shining Brass was the code name given to U.S. Army Special Forces cross-border recon missions and raids into where, beginning in 1965?

ANS: Laos.

143 What famous nickname did the press gave to the purloined *History of the U.S. Decision-Making Process in Vietnam?*
 a) the Quill Memorandum
 b) the Pickwick Papers
 c) the Pentagon Papers
 d) the Ellsberg Document

ANS: c.

144 What countries were expected to be the first and the last "dominoes" of Southeast Asia?

ANS: South Vietnam and Australia.

145 Which U.S. President first enunciated the Domino Theory?

ANS: President Eisenhower, in an April 7, 1954, speech.

146 In Ike's administration, who was Christian Herter?

ANS: He was secretary of state from April 1959 to January 1961, when the NLF was formed and U.S. advisers were first sent to Vietnam.

147 What American Catholic Cardinal had Ngo Dinh Diem as his protégé?
 a) Cushing
 b) Spellman
 c) Menzies

ANS: b.

148 This British counterinsurgency adviser defeated the Communist insurgency in Malaysia during the Eisenhower years and was held in awe by subsequent U.S. administrations, which continuously sought his advice on Vietnam.

   a) Edward D. Lansdale
   b) Lucien G. Conein
   c) Samuel L. Popkin
   d) John Paul Vann
   e) Robert K. Thompson

ANS: e.

149 When did Edward Lansdale arrive in Vietnam, and why?

ANS: President Eisenhower sent Lansdale to run the Saigon Military Mission, which was responsible for formulating counterinsurgency plans for South Vietnam and for conducting sabotage raids into North Vietnam. The year was 1954.

150 True or false: Lansdale originally built his counterinsurgency reputation in Thailand.

ANS: False. Lansdale defeated the Communist-led Huk Rebellion in the Philippines after World War II.

151 At what year do the names of Vietnam War dead inscribed on the Vietnam War Memorial in Washington begin?

ANS: 1959.

152 At what year do they end?

ANS: 1975.

153   What is the exact number of Americans killed in Vietnam?
- a) 35,201
- b) 46,300
- c) 57,939
- d) 58,130
- e) 63,455

ANS: d.

3

UNITS AND INSIGNIA

1 What U.S. headquarters command was known as "Pentagon East"?

ANS: MACV, or Military Assistance Command, Vietnam, the central command for U.S. forces in Vietnam located at Tan San Nhut airfield.

2 Who or what was ARVN?

ANS: South Vietnamese Armed Forces (Armed Forces of Vietnam).

3 Who were the Screaming Eagles?
   a) First Air Cavalry
   b) 101st Airborne
   c) Phantom jet fighters

ANS: b.

FACT

The 101st Airborne gained its fame during World War II, when its commander, surrounded by German troops at Bastogne, replied to a demand for surrender with the answer, "Nuts."

---

4   What was III MAF (pronounced "Three Maf")?

ANS: Third Marine Amphibious Force.

5   Who were the "SEABEEs"?

ANS: U.S. Navy combat construction battalions (C.B.'s), although they also came in regiment- and brigade-size units.

6   What unit's troops wore a yellow shoulder patch with a horse's head on it?

ANS: First Air Calvary.

7   What does MI stand for?
  a) multiple insurgencies
  b) mechanical interception
  c) military intelligence

ANS: c.

8   The major U.S. ground units in northern South Vietnam were
  a) Marines
  b) Army airborne troops
  c) Army tank units

ANS: a.

9 **What was the Vietnam Service Medal awarded for?**

ANS: It was awarded for serving at least one day in Vietnam or on board a Navy ship or Air Force plane supporting the war effort between July 3, 1965, and March 28, 1973.

10 **What badge consisted of a rifle enclosed in a rectangular box atop a wreath?**

ANS: The Combat Infantryman's Badge (CIB).

11 **How did a soldier earn a CIB?**

ANS: By serving in a unit that came under fire in combat or by working with a South Vietnamese unit that took part directly in the fighting.

12 **How many Army and Marine divisions fought in Vietnam?**

ANS: Seven Army divisions—First Cavalry, First Infantry, Fourth Infantry, Ninth Infantry, Americal (Twenty-third) Infantry, Twenty-fifth Infantry, and 101st Airborne. In addition, there were two division-size Army brigades, Fifth Infantry and Eighty-second Airborne. There were two Marine divisions—the First and Third—in Vietnam, as well as regiments from the Fifth Marines.

13 **How many South Vietnamese divisions fought in the war?**

ANS: Eleven.

14 **How many North Vietnamese divisions?**

ANS: Twenty-one.

15 Two army units had the designation Eighteenth, and both were in Vietnam. But they had entirely different functions. What were the units?

ANS: The Eighteenth Engineer Brigade and the Eighteenth MP Brigade.

16 Describe the distinctive insignia of the Eighty-second Airborne Division.

ANS: A circle surrounded by a square in which two A's mirror each other. On top of the square is a semicircular patch inscribed *Airborne*.

17 What was known as the Blackhorse Regiment?

ANS: The Eleventh Armored Cavalry Regiment, which started out as a horse cavalry unit in 1901 and by World War II was a mechanized outfit. Its insignia was a rearing black stallion in front of a red and white shield.

18 Describe the Fifth Special Forces insignia.

ANS: A gold sword with three lightning rods across it, in a spade-shaped blue patch.

19 By what famous nickname are the Special Forces more commonly known?

ANS: The Green Berets.

20 In the Army, companies are usually divided into platoons and squads, except for the Green Berets. What were they divided into?

ANS: Detachments and teams.

21 What teams were given "project" names like Delta, Omega, Sigma, and Gamma?

ANS: Highly classified Green Beret units.

22 Why were they so highly classified?

ANS: They operated secretly in Cambodia, Laos, and North Vietnam.

23 Who killed Thai Khac Chuyen?

ANS: According to the Army, Special Forces Col. Robert Rheault, commander of the Fifth Special Forces, killed this alleged double agent, who was working for his unit.

24 What happened to Rheault?

ANS: The case was dismissed for reasons of national security on September 29, 1969.

25 What U.S. President was enamored of the Green Berets?

ANS: John F. Kennedy.

26 What was the early principal mission of the Green Berets in Vietnam?

ANS: To work with Vietnamese units in forming their own defensive organizations to fight the Vietcong. The Green Berets paid particular attention to the so-called Montagnard tribesmen in the strategic Central Highlands, who were looked down on by the Vietnamese.

27 What was one of the first units to arrive in—and the last to leave—Vietnam and eventually became one of the largest commands in Vietnam, with 24,000 men and 4,230 aircraft?

ANS: The First Aviation Brigade.

28 Describe the First Aviation Brigade's insignia.

ANS: A fierce-looking bird with wings extended, perching on the handle of an upright sword.

29 What Army unit was sometimes called the Blanket Division?

ANS: The First Air Cavalry Division.

30 What unit's patch had a big red number one on it?

ANS: The U.S. Army's First Infantry Division.

31 True or false: The First Infantry Division was called The Big Red One because it was the first Army division to arrive in Vietnam, in October 1965.

ANS: Its name is inspired by the design of its unit patch, a big red 1.

32 What was the First Log?

ANS: The First Logistical Command was the main support group for U.S. troops, transporting ammunition, storing supplies, ammo, and fuel, and operating mortuaries in Saigon and Da Nang.

33 True or false: All U.S. military personnel in Vietnam wore uniforms.

ANS: False. Some intelligence personnel wore civilian clothes.

34 Who were the only U.S. soldiers to drive black jeeps in Vietnam?

ANS: U.S. intelligence personnel.

35 What did CID stand for?

ANS: Criminal Investigation Detachment—the Army's detectives.

36 What was the ONI?

ANS: The Office of Naval Investigations—the Navy's intelligence arm.

37 What was the NIS?

ANS: The Naval Investigative Service—the Navy's detectives.

38 What was the 525th MI Group?

ANS: The Army's principal intelligence-gathering organization in Vietnam.

39 What was the Ponderosa?
a) a ranch in the A Shau Valley
b) a French plantation in the Delta
c) a French villa turned into a bar at military intelligence headquarters in Saigon
d) a secret landing field for herbicide operations in the Central Highlands
e) the enlisted men's bar in Pleiku

ANS: c.

40 What was an I/T?

ANS: A Vietnamese working as an interpreter/translator.

41 What was a CI team?
a) a combat infantry team
b) a command intelligence team
c) a counterintelligence team

ANS: c.

42 What was a generals' mess?

ANS: The eating place for general officers.

43 What famous club did the sun set in the east behind in the movie *The Green Berets*?

ANS: The Navy Officers Club in Da Nang.

44 What is the Marine motto?
a) "Do or die."
b) "Never quit."

c) "Straight ahead."
d) "Always faithful."

ANS: d.

45 On the First Marine Division's insignia is written a word commemorating what memorable battle?
a) Ticonderoga
b) Shiloh
c) Alamo
d) Bulge
e) Midway
f) Guadalcanal
g) Inchon
h) Managua

ANS: f.

46 What is the nickname of the First Marine Division?

ANS: The Old Breed.

47 This unit's nickname is Ivy, which comes from the Roman numeral IV. Sometimes it was called the Poison Ivy Division, the Famous Fourth, or in Vietnam, the Funky Fourth. What was it?

ANS: The Fourth Army Division.

48 What is the greatest medal that the nation can award for valor in battle?

ANS: The Medal of Honor.

49 How many Medals of Honor were awarded during Vietnam?

ANS: 239: 155 in the Army, 57 in the Marines, 15 in the Navy, and 12 in the Air Force.

50 What is the nation's second-highest award for bravery, awarded by the Navy and Marine Corps for extraordinary heroism in action against the enemy?
   a) the Marine Cross
   b) the Croix de Guerre
   c) the Navy Cross

ANS: c.

51 A bronze star is awarded for meritorious service by the Army, and a silver star for heroism in combat. Who gets a gold star?

ANS: A woman whose son died in battle.

52 In Vietnam, soldiers called it the Flower Power Unit or the Psychedelic Cookie because of its insignia, an eight-petaled flower. What was the unit?

ANS: The Ninth Infantry Division, also known as the Old Reliables.

53 What airborne unit's casualties in Vietnam were even greater than the losses of either the Eighty-second or the 101st Airborne division in Europe in World War II? Its insignia portrays a winged figure encircling a sword with the word Airborne atop the patch.

ANS: The 173d Airborne Brigade.

54 This country's elite unit was sent to Vietnam in 1967. It was called the Queen's Cobras. What country did it come from?
   a) Thailand
   b) Philippines
   c) Taiwan
   d) South Korea
   e) North Korea

ANS: a.

55 What country sent its SAS units to Vietnam?

ANS: Australia.

56 True or false: Only the United States gave its soldiers a fixed tour in Vietnam.

ANS: False. Australian troops also served a fixed tour.

57 Which branch of the U.S. service served a thirteen-month tour?

ANS: The Marines.

58 What did R&R stand for?
   a) rest and recuperation
   b) rest and relaxation
   c) rocking and rolling
   d) reconnaisance and recon

ANS: b.

59 Of the following cities, one was not an R&R destination for American soldiers during the Vietnam war:
   a) Tokyo

  b) Bangkok
  c) Manila
  d) Phnom Penh
  e) Kuala Lampur
  f) Taipei
  g) Honolulu
  h) Sydney
  i) Penang

ANS: d.

60 What nickname was given to the outdoor sidewalk café of the Hotel Continental in Saigon by its patrons?

ANS: The Continental Shelf.

61 Who were the Redcatchers?

ANS: The 199th Infantry Brigade, which was activated at Fort Benning in June 1966 for Vietnam duty. Its shoulder patch was a flaming spear.

62 Describe the distinctive SEABEEs insignia.

ANS: A flying bee with a rivet gun over the word *SEABEEs*.

63 Who were the SEALs?

ANS: Navy commandos who operated behind enemy lines: *Sea-Air-Land* gives it the acronym.

64 What Air Force outfit had overall responsibility for coordinating the U.S. air war in South Vietnam?

ANS: The Seventh Air Force.

65   What Marine division was the first to land in Vietnam, in March 1965? Its insignia is a three-sided star in a triangular patch.

ANS: The Third Marine Division.

66   What foreign nation sent its Tiger Division to South Vietnam?

ANS: South Korea.

67   What unit's nickname is Tropic Lightning?

ANS: The Twenty-fifth Infantry Division. It was in Hawaii at the time of Pearl Harbor and saw service throughout the Pacific in World War II, in Korea, and then in Vietnam.

68   What was the Twenty-fifth's insignia?

ANS: A lightning bolt inside an oak-leaf-shaped patch.

69   What is a V device?
   a) a bent metal rod to affix plastique explosives
   b) a tripod for a small rocket
   c) an attachment to a medal denoting *valor*

ANS: c.

70   What was the nickname of the South Korean Ninth Infantry Division?
   a) Black Horse
   b) White Horse

    c) Spotted Horse
    d) Horse's Neck
    e) Horse's Ass

ANS: b.

4

WEAPONS

1 The defoliant Agent Orange was sprayed over South Vietnam between March 1965 and June 1970. How many millions of gallons were dropped?
   a) 10 to 20
   b) 20 to 30
   c) 50 to 75
   d) over 100

ANS: a (11.3).

2 How was it disseminated?

ANS: By C-123 aircraft.

3 What color was Agent Orange?
   a) white
   b) colorless
   c) orange
   d) reddish-brown

ANS: d.

4   Why was it called Agent Orange?

ANS: Because of the orange stripe on the fifty-five-gallon drums in which it was stored.

5   Aside from Agent Orange, there were five additional herbicidal agents employed in Vietnam. What were they?

ANS: White, Blue, Purple, Pink, and Green.

6   What was the difference among them?

ANS: The degree of destructive capability.

7   What was the objective of spraying herbicides?

ANS: To destroy crops and jungle foliage that hid or supported Vietcong.

8   When was its peak use in South Vietnam?

ANS: In 1967, when nearly 1.5 million acres were defoliated, including 221,000 acres of crops.

9   True or false: Conclusive evidence has linked exposure to Agent Orange with birth defects, cancer, and even death.

ANS: False. By mid-1986, the evidence, although persuasive, was still inconclusive.

10   Was the Agent Orange spraying program considered a strategic success?

ANS: No. Although occasionally successful in a tactical sense, it became a public relations disaster when it was discovered, and it thus contributed to the undermining of public support for the war.

11 **What were Dixie Station and Yankee Station?**

ANS: Patrol areas for U.S. warships in the Tonkin Gulf of the South China Sea, off Vietnam.

12 **U.S. aircraft carriers served a key purpose throughout the war. How many different ones were stationed there during the war?**

ANS: Nineteen.

13 **Of the following four carriers, which were named after sites of past U.S. military glories?**
   a) **Yorktown**
   b) **Ticonderoga**
   c) **Midway**
   d) **Coral Sea**

ANS: All of the above.

14 **Name the preferred rifle of the North Vietnamese and the Vietcong.**

ANS: AK-47.

15 **The inventor of the AK-47 also gave his name to another assault rifle. Was it**
   a) **Khrushchev**
   b) **Malinkov**
   c) **Dobrinan**
   d) **Kalashnikov**
   e) **Baryshnikov**

ANS: d.

16 What was the rifle caliber of the AK-47?

ANS: 7.62.

17 For what two reasons did the Vietcong love the introduction of American M-16 rifle to Vietnam?

ANS: Captured M-16 ammo could be fired in an AK-47 (but not vice versa), and the M-16 was lighter than the AK-47.

18 Did the U.S. Army employ tank units in Vietnam?

ANS: Yes, three Army battalions and one Marine tank battalion.

19 Did the Communists deploy their own tanks in Vietnam?

ANS: Yes.

20 When was the first Communist use of tanks?

ANS: In February 1968, when thirteen PT-76 amphibious tanks overran a Special Forces camp at Lang Vei, near Khe Sanh. Tanks were also used extensively during the Easter Offensive of 1972, in which they employed the heavier T-54s, and during the final offensive of 1975, when over seven hundred tanks were massed for the assault on Saigon.

21 The U.S. Cavalry extensively used the M-113 vehicle. What was its more familiar name?

ANS: Armored personnel carrier, or APC.

22   Artillery has been called "the king of battle." If so, what is infantry?

ANS: The queen of battle.

23   What special U.S. artillery shell, designed to be used against a mass infantry attack, contains thousands of tiny steel arrows called "flechettes"?
   a) beehive
   b) fragger
   c) dart cannon
   d) claymore

ANS: a.

Match the following aircraft bomber designations with their names:

24	A-26	a) stratofortress
25	B-52	b) canberra
26	B-57	c) air commando

ANS: 24-c, 25-a, 26-b.

27   Artillery use is measured by shells; bombs are measured by tonnage. How many more tons of bombs were dropped on Indochina by Air Force bombers alone than the 2.15 million tons that were delivered to targets by all U.S. forces during World War II?
   a) 4.1 million
   b) 6.1 million
   c) 8.1 million
   d) 10.1 million

ANS: b.

28   What was a pungi stake, and how did it work?

ANS: It was a green bamboo stalk sharpened to a deadly point and buried by the Vietcong in pits, tips turned upward, along jungle trails.

29 True or false: The pungi stake, although colorfully notorious, was rarely used by the Communists.

ANS: False. Pungi stakes and other booby traps accounted for about 11 percent of all deaths and 17 percent of all U.S. wounds in Vietnam.

30 What was a claymore?

ANS: A United States–made remote-control antipersonnel land mine.

31 What was a cobra?

ANS: An attack helicopter.

32 Did the Communists use attack helicopters during the war?

ANS: No.

33 What did the United States use dogs for in Vietnam?

ANS: To sniff out weapons caches and track enemy soldiers.

34 What did the United States use geese for in Vietnam?

ANS: To guard bridges.

35 What was a free-fire zone?

ANS: A zone where the United States employed unrestricted firepower.

36 What was H&I fire?

ANS: Literally, harrassment and interdiction artillery fire. In practice, it was the kind of shooting employed in free-fire zones.

37 What was a Huey?

ANS: A UH-1A or UH-1B assault transport helicopter.

38 What was a Jolly Green Giant?

ANS: The CH-54, a flying crane.

39 Were any helicopters lost over North Vietnam?

ANS: Yes, ten.

40 Were helicopters reliable?

ANS: 2,566 crashed in accidents; 2,066 were shot down.

41 What kind of weapon did a door gunner fire?

ANS: A M-60 machine gun.

42 What were Kit Carson scouts?

ANS: Former Vietcong who were employed as guides and interpreters with forward allied combat units.

43 What weapon was known by the acronym LAW?

ANS: The M-72 light antitank weapon.

44 What was a lurp?

ANS: A soldier on long range patrols (LRP) deep into enemy territory.

45 What was the standard U.S. infantry weapon at the start of the Vietnam War?
  a) M-1
  b) M-7
  c) M-12
  d) M-14
  e) M-16

ANS: d.

46 What U.S. shoulder weapon, which looked like a fattened-up shotgun and was first used in Vietnam, fired 40mm grenade cartridges?

ANS: The M-79 grenade launcher.

47 What were the standard Soviet- and Chinese-supplied mortars used by the Vietcong?
  a) 60mm
  b) 80mm
  c) 4.2-inch
  d) 120mm
  e) 82mm

ANS: d and e.

48 What were the three kinds of rockets employed by the Vietcong?

ANS: 107mm, 122mm, 140mm.

49 What was the maximum range of the Communist 140mm rocket?

ANS: 11 km.

50 True or false: The United States' and Saigon's were the only military forces using napalm during the war.

ANS: False. The Communists used napalm in flamethrowers.

51 The shells fired by offshore U.S. warships were sometimes as heavy as
   a) cement mixers
   b) grand pianos
   c) Volkswagens
   d) Pontiacs
   e) limousines

ANS: c (2,000 pounds).

52 True or false: No U.S. ships cruising offshore were sunk by the Communists during the entire Vietnam War.

ANS: True. One destroyer was hit by a MiG and sixteen were hit by shore batteries, but none were sunk.

53 What did the United States mainly use parachutes for in Vietnam?

ANS: Dropping supplies to forward units.

54 What were Pathfinder soldiers, also known as Black Hats?

ANS: They were airborne infantrymen who were deposited behind enemy lines to reconnoiter landing areas.

55 What were phosphorous grenades used for?

ANS: To mark ground positions.

56 What was a Bouncing Betty?

ANS: A buried landmine that jumped into the air and exploded when tripped.

57 Who were the Rangers?

ANS: Graduates of a special warfare school at Fort Benning who specialized in long-range patrols.

58 What were Rome Plows?

ANS: Large tractors with special heavy blades for combat landclearing tasks, built by the Rome Caterpillar Company of Georgia.

59 What was an RPG?

ANS: A rocket-propelled grenade used by Communist forces. The RPG-7 was a later model with twice the range and penetration power.

60 SAM is a man's name, but what kind of weapon is it?

ANS: A surface-to-air missile—usually a Communist-bloc designation.

61 True or false: Even though the United States controlled the skies over Vietnam, it had at its disposal HAWK surface-to-air missiles in case of MiG attacks.

ANS: True, but they were eventually withdrawn.

62 The Russians gave Hanoi SAM-2 missiles to defend itself. What were SAM-2s for?

ANS: To shoot down B-52 bombers (the two-and-a-half-ton missiles had a range of about nineteen nautical miles and 85,000 feet).

63 A small, hand-held SA-7 Strella was introduced in 1972 and used against what?

ANS: Lower-flying planes and helicopters.

64 What was/is a sapper?

ANS: The usual designation of explosive-carrying Communist commandos.

65 What was a Gooney Bird?

ANS: The C-47, a twin-propeller workhorse transport plane.

66   When the Gooney Bird was lethally armed, what were its designation and nickname?

ANS: The AC-47, "Puff the Magic Dragon."

5

THE GROUND WAR

1 When was the first U.S. officer killed in Vietnam, and what was his name?

ANS: September 2, 1945; Captain Peter Stone.

2 Stone worked for the World War II–era secret intelligence service of the U.S. What was its name?

ANS: O.S.S., Office of Strategic Services.

3 The O.S.S. team's operations were run from:
   a) Kunming, China
   b) Tokyo
   c) Hanoi

ANS: a.

4 At the end of World War II, what happened when Ho wrote to President Truman asking for continued support in his fight to keep the French from returning as rulers of Vietnam?

ANS: Truman ignored him.

5 True or false: President Roosevelt favored United States military aid to the French effort to reestablish control over Indochina.

ANS: False.

6 What percentage of the French military effort was borne financially by U.S. taxpayers by 1954?
   a) 20
   b) 40
   c) 60
   d) 80

ANS: d.

7 What happened at Dienbienphu?

ANS: The French were routed by the Viet Minh there on May 7, 1954. The shock of this defeat pushed France into a peace conference at Geneva.

8 Who was the supreme Viet Minh military commander at Dienbienphu?

ANS: Vo Nguyen Giap.

9 What extraordinary military weapon did the United States consider using at Dienbienphu?

ANS: The atomic bomb.

10 What U.S. President first sent military advisers to South Vietnam, and when?

ANS: Eisenhower, in February 1955.

11 When CIA pilot Francis Gary Powers was shot down over Russia, in May 1960, how many U.S. advisers were in Vietnam?

ANS: 685.

12 And how many a year later, in all?

ANS: A little over 1,000.

13 What new and startling U.S. weapon arrived in Vietnam in December 1961?
 a) the M-60 machine gun
 b) the M-16 automatic rifle
 c) the M-79 grenade launcher
 d) "Puff the Magic Dragon"
 e) the helicopter gunship

ANS: e.

14 True or false: There were no more than 1,000 U.S. military personnel stationed in South Vietnam by the end of 1961.

ANS: False. There were 2,600.

15 What devastating U.S. weapon arrived in the skies over Vietnam in January 1962?
 a) dry ice
 b) Agent Orange
 c) dirigibles
 d) cluster bombs
 e) forward air controllers

ANS: b.

16   By the end of 1963, how many U.S. advisers were in Vietnam?

ANS: 17,000.

17   Related to Vietnam, what is dioxin?

ANS: The lethal chemical component in the herbicide Agent Orange.

18   By the end of 1964, how many U.S. troops were in Vietnam?

ANS: 23,300.

19   What did U.S. commanders decide the Vietcong military strategy was by late 1964?
   a) capture Saigon
   b) capture major coastal cities
   c) cut South Vietnam in half
   d) control the skies
   e) control rice-growing areas

ANS: c.

20   Who became known to critics and fans alike as "Blow Torch" for his aggressive approach to "pacification"?

ANS: Robert Komer of the CIA.

21   Who ran the Phoenix assassination program?

ANS: William Colby, who became CIA director in 1973.

22 The boots GIs wore in Vietnam were a radical departure from past army footwear. What made them different?

ANS: "Jungle boots" had nylon instead of leather tops and had a thin steel plate embedded in the sole.

23 What regional "allies" sent combat troops to Vietnam in support of the United States?

ANS: South Korea sent the Tiger Division, the Blue Dragon Brigade, the White Horse Infantry Division, the Capital Division, and the Ninth Infantry Brigade. Australia sent its First Battalion, the Royal Australian Regiment, and the First Australian Task Force, augmented by a Special Air Service squadron of commandos. New Zealand sent an artillery battery, Bangkok sent the Royal Thai Army Volunteer Force (11,500 men), and the Philippines sent a construction battalion.

24 What does KIA mean?

ANS: Killed in action.

25 That was easy. What did TAOR mean?

ANS: The Tactical Area of Responsibility for a U.S. combat unit.

26 What was the fastest means of transportation to get to battle for U.S. troops?

ANS: Helicopter.

27 A designation of a U.S. helicopter was always preceded by the letters *CH*. What did they mean?

ANS: Chinook, its manufacturer.

28 How many propeller blades did the workhorse CH-47 have?

ANS: 6.

29 U.S. strategists adopted a program of relocating peasants into what?

ANS: "Strategic hamlets."

30 Actually, this program had been tried earlier without much success under a different name. What was it?

ANS: "New Life" (Ap Moi) hamlets.

31 The Vietnamese name for the program to encourage Vietcong defections was called
   a) Phuong Hoang
   b) Xin Loi
   c) Chieu Hoi
   d) Lai Day
   e) Chao Ong

ANS: c.

32 According to U.S. figures, how many Vietcong soldiers deserted between 1963 and 1973?
   a) 160,000
   b) 250,000
   c) 385,000
   d) 1,000,000
   e) 2,000,000

ANS: a.

33 It didn't take long for U.S. troops to learn to decline offers of soft drinks from Vietnamese children. Why?

ANS: They were often filled with acid or broken glass.

34 In the history of U.S. involvement in Vietnam, what is important about March 8, 1965?

ANS: On that day, the first contingent of Marines—3,500 troops—arrived in Vietnam.

35 Their mission was to
   a) guard the Da Nang airfield
   b) secure the city of Da Nang
   c) pacify surrounding hamlets
   d) kill as many Vietcong as possible
   e) set up a television station

ANS: a.

36 When did U.S. soldiers become eligible for combat pay?

ANS: In April 1965, retroactive to January 1965.

37 What was the first U.S. Army ground combat unit to arrive in Vietnam in May 1965?
   a) 165th Infantry
   b) 101st Airborne
   c) 173d Airborne
   d) USARV
   e) MACV

ANS: c.

38   As early as April 1963, the United States began to construct a huge, deep water port on South Vietnam's coast. What was its name?

ANS: Cam Ranh Bay.

39   By mid-1965, how many U.S. troops were in Vietnam?

ANS: 75,000.

40   Where and when was the first officially announced "search and destroy mission" involving a major U.S. unit?

ANS: In War Zone D, northwest of Saigon, the 173rd Airborne Division launched a series of sweeping attacks against the Vietcong. It was on June 28–30, 1965.

41   How many Americans had died in Vietnam by this time (between 1961 and mid-1965)?

ANS: 503, with 2,270 wounded.

42   How many POWs were there by 1965?

ANS: Fifty-seven.

43   In November 1965, the Marines launched Operation Piranha against the Vietcong First Regiment at Cape Batangan. Where was that?

ANS: On the sandy coastal plain south of Da Nang.

44   What big battle in October–November 1965 prevented the Communists from slicing the top third off South Vietnam?

ANS: The Battle of the Ia Drang Valley.

45 What was the tactical significance of that battle for the United States?

ANS: It was the first time the United States and the Communists engaged in a set piece battle between main force units—something the United States had long sought as advantageous to its traditional style of fighting.

46 What was the principal U.S. unit in the Ia Drang?

ANS: The First Cavalry Division.

47 What special award did LBJ bestow on that unit for its conduct in the battle?

ANS: The Presidential Unit Citation.

48 What is the significance of that?

ANS: It was the only such award presented during the whole war in Vietnam.

FACT

The U.S. Army's First Cavalry Division was formed from a number of horse cavalry elements in 1921. By World War II, the division had been transformed into a footsoldier outfit. The Cav fought throughout the southern Pacific and had the honor of being the first U.S. division to land in Japan in 1945. The Cav also fought in Korea, and in July 1965 it was made into the Army's First Cavalry Division. Two months later, the Cav moved into Vietnam. The Cav fought throughout Vietnam, and its soldiers won twenty-five Congressional Medals of Honor. More than 30,000 Cav soldiers were killed or wounded in Vietnam before most of the division left Vietnam in April 1970. The Cav, now stationed at Fort Hood, Texas, has once again been transformed. In its latest incarnation it is a mechanized mobile unit.

---

49 How many U.S. troops were stationed in Vietnam in 1965?

ANS: 184,300.

50 In May 1966, U.S. commanders noted an ominous development in Communist military strategy. What was it?

ANS: The buildup of North Vietnamese forces—10,000 men—across the DMZ from South Vietnam.

51 What was Westmoreland's reaction?

ANS: He asked for more troops.

52 The United States and South Vietnam then launched the largest combined offensive of the war to that date in order to destroy the massed Communist troops. Its name was
  a) Operation Hayseed
  b) Operation Hastings
  c) Rolling Thunder
  d) Homecoming
  e) Oplan 34A

ANS: b.

53 This North Vietnamese unit arrived in South Vietnam in the summer of 1966 and stayed to fight until the end of the war. What was the unit?

ANS: The 324B Steel Regiment.

54 What was the Iron Triangle?

ANS: The impenetrable and heavily forested area twenty-five miles northwest of Saigon, controlled by the Communists.

55 In August 1966, the President ordered two large Army combat units into Vietnam from stateside. What were they?
  a) the First Infantry Division
  b) the Fourth Infantry Division
  c) the Ninth Infantry Division
  d) the 101st Airborne Brigade
  e) the 196th Light Infantry Brigade

ANS: b and e.

56 True or false: The 101st Airborne Brigade was parachuted into South Vietnam.

ANS: False.

57 With other units, the Fourth Infantry was quickly commanded to protect what strategically crucial small city in the Central Highlands?

ANS: Pleiku.

58 How many U.S. troops were stationed in Vietnam by the end of 1966?

ANS: 385,300.

59 How many GIs had been killed in Vietnam by then?
a) 3,322
b) 4,433
c) 5,544
d) 6,644

ANS: d.

60 In January 1967, the United States launched an ambitious operation northwest of Saigon called Cedar Falls. What was its objective?

ANS: To attack Communist strongholds in the Iron Triangle.

61 Can you name any of the five U.S. Army units involved in Cedar Falls?

ANS: The Eleventh Armored Cavalry Regiment, the 173d Airborne Brigade, plus elements of the Twenty-fifth Infantry Division, the 196th Light Infantry, and the First Infantry Division.

62 A young lieutenant colonel, later to become secretary of state, commanded a battalion of the First Division against Ben Tre in that operation. His name?

ANS: Alexander Haig.

63 Which of the units engaged in Operation Cedar Falls was nicknamed The Big Red One?

ANS: The First Infantry Division.

64 What U.S. unit was nicknamed The Herd?

ANS: The 173d Airborne.

65 Did the *airborne* designation mean those U.S. troops parachuted into battle in Vietnam?

ANS: No. In actuality, it meant they were helicoptered into battle.

66 In June 1967, one of the most violent battles of the Vietnam War began in the rugged Central Highlands of Kontum Province. Like most famous battles, it became known for its principal location. Can you name it?
  a) Ban Me Thuot
  b) Con Thien
  c) Dak To
  d) Cam Lo
  e) Dong Ha

ANS: c.

67 This struggle of the giants, which lasted almost six months into December 1967, became known as
  a) the Battle for the Highlands
  b) Westmoreland's Last Stand
  c) Hamburger Hills
  d) the Beginning of the End
  e) the Battle of the Bulge

ANS: a.

68 Which side lost forty helicopters?

ANS: Only the American–Saigon side had helicopters.

69 After more than five months of fighting, the Communist units withdrew. Where to?

ANS: Laos and Cambodia.

70 The U.S. Navy conducted assault operations in the vast network of rivers and streams of the Mekong Delta. What were the Navy forces called?

ANS: Mobile Riverine Forces.

71 What was the acronym of the Navy's version of Green Berets?

ANS: SEALs (for Sea, Air, and Land).

72 One bright young Navy lieutenant who earned Purple Hearts and other awards for gallantry with the riverine units later became a U.S. senator from Massachusetts. What was his name?
   a) Lodge
   b) Kerry
   c) Kennedy

ANS: b.

73 Operation Junction City, in March 1967, was the largest and next-to-last big operation of the war. What was its objective?

ANS: To destroy COSVN, the Central Office for South Vietnam, headquarters for the Communist military in the south.

74 A month later, General Westmoreland visited Washington with one major objective. What did he want?

ANS: More troops—a minimum of 80,500, a maximum of 200,000 more.

75 What was the one military operation in which U.S. airborne troops were parachuted into the battle zone?

ANS: Operation Junction City. One battalion—the Second battalion, 503d Infantry of the 173d Airborne Brigade—out of the twenty-two U.S. and four South Vietnamese battalions involved in the operation, was dropped deep into the jungle near Cambodia from the air.

76 On February 22, 1967, during Operation Junction City, one of the largest helicopter lifts in the history of modern warfare took place. How many choppers were used in the operation that day?

ANS: 249.

77 During Operation Junction City, the 173d Airborne discovered the headquarters of one of the Vietcong's main offices. What was it?

ANS: The Vietcong Central Information Office.

78 Another big U.S. offensive, which began in May 1967 and continued for the rest of the year, utilized constant day-and-night forays by small units to improve security around Saigon. Can you name that operation?

ANS: Operation Fairfax.

79 There was always a ferocious debate inside the military over the relative merits of big unit operations (favored by General Westmoreland) and small unit operations. What was the immediate, personal advantage to U.S. troops of small unit operations?

ANS: There were more Communist casualties per U.S. casualty.

80   The Twenty-third Infantry Division was formed for combat operations in northern South Vietnam. It became notorious for taking and giving out combat punishment. It was called "Amer----" Division.

ANS: The Americal Division.

81   What did that name mean? Was it
a) an "air cavalry" unit
b) composed mostly of boys from California
c) more patriotic than others

ANS: None of the above. The original Americal Division was formed during World War II by U.S. Army units on the Pacific island of New Caledonia. The Vietnam version of it was created to reflect the Marine Corps' and Army's working relationship in Vietnam.

82   By December 1967, how many U.S. troops were in Vietnam?
a) about 250,000
b) twice that
c) much less than 250,000 (because of the peace movement's influence)
d) 600,000

ANS: b (485,600).

83   1967 saw the continued escalation of U.S. troop strength in Vietnam. Casualties also kept climbing. How many Americans were killed in Vietnam that year?
a) 2,000
b) 5,000
c) 9,000
d) 12,000

ANS: c (9,377).

84 U.S. special warfare units, known by their acronym, SOG, were sent where for secret reconnaissance of the Ho Chi Minh Trail?

ANS: Laos.

85 General Westmoreland moved his Special Forces teams out of Khe Sanh and down the road to Lang Vei in late 1966. Who replaced them at Khe Sanh?

ANS: The Marines.

86 The first major contact with the enemy around Khe Sanh occurred in April 1967. Out of it arose great controversy about the M-16 rifle. What happened?

ANS: Dozens of the Marines died in Communist ambushes when their M-16s failed to fire.

87 What was the design predecessor of the M-16 called, and who designed it?

ANS: The AR-15, designed by Eugene Stoner for the Armilite Corporation in the late 1950s.

FACT _____

The AR-15 was a perfectly fine weapon. Early Special Forces soldiers in Vietnam preferred it so much to the M-14 that they bought them on the black market, with money out of their own pockets, for six hundred dollars apiece. Gen. Curtis LeMay equipped his special air police with AR-15s. It wasn't until the Pentagon began to tinker with the AR-15 that it fell into disrepute. Desk-bound army officers decided to use the Mathieson gunpowder, normally used in .30-caliber bullets for the standard-issue M-14, for the AR-15. This made the AR-15's .22-caliber bullets both too powerful and too dirty for rapid fire. The rifle would jam just when a GI needed it the most. The result was a weapon so unreliable that soldiers struggled to keep their M-14s. Soldiers began pleading for changes in the weapon by letter to their congressional representatives. Only after reports surfaced of GIs dying with cleaning rods and AR-15s in their hands did the Pentagon redesign the rifle.

---

88 What was Operation Scotland?

ANS: The defense of Khe Sanh.

89 Some six thousand U.S. Marines and South Vietnamese troops defended Khe Sanh. What units were they from?

ANS: The Third Marine Division's Twenty-sixth Regiment, battalions from the Ninth and Thirteenth Marine Regiments, and the South Vietnamese Thirty-seventh Ranger Battalion.

90 The massive U.S. bombing campaign around Khe Sanh was aptly named after a famous tourist spot on the United States-Canada border. What was it?

ANS: Niagara.

91 The site of the battle for Khe Sanh was often compared with the site of what other famous battle in Vietnam? Why?

ANS: Dienbienphu. Like that valley plateau in northern Tonkin where the Viet Minh overwhelmed the French in 1954, Khe Sanh was a remote, heavily fortified position near Laos in a valley surrounded by North Vietnamese troops and artillery.

92 What was the principal U.S. weapon used at Khe Sanh?

ANS: The B-52 bomber. Groups of six flew over NVA positions every three hours around the clock, dropping a total of 75,000 tons of bombs in more than 2,600 sorties.

93 Elements of what Army units were finally sent to open up the road to Khe Sanh from the east?

ANS: The First Air Cavalry, along with elements of the First Marine Division and the South Vietnamese Airborne Brigade.

94 True or false: The total number of Americans killed at Khe Sanh was infinitesimal compared to Communist casualties.

ANS: True. The official count of U.S. KIAs was 205. North Vietnamese losses were estimated at 10–15,000.

95 What finally happened at Khe Sanh in June 1968?

ANS: The base was abandoned by U.S. forces.

96 The Vietnamese holiday of Tet celebrates what event?

ANS: The beginning of the lunar new year in late January–early February.

97 In Chinese-Vietnamese calendar symbolism, 1968 was the year of the
a) goat
b) monkey
c) dog
d) pig
e) cock

ANS: b.

98 The Communists launched major attacks against what percentage of South Vietnam's forty-four provincial capitals in the Tet Offensive?
 a) 25
 b) 33
 c) 75
 d) 100

ANS: c.

99 What was the principal weapon of the Vietcong at Tet?

ANS: Surprise.

100 For most Americans who watched the 1968 Tet attacks on television, one temporary Vietcong success was profoundly shocking. What was it?

ANS: The invasion of the U.S. Embassy grounds in Saigon.

101 The opening move of the Communists in the Tet attacks was badly botched. What was it?

ANS: In the 2 A.M., January 31 sapper attack on the ARVN General Joint Staff compound in Saigon, a U.S. jeep patrol accidently arrived on the scene.

FACT _____

One of the strangest events in the annals of Tet 1968 was the Vietcong attack on Ba Tho District Headquarters south of Quang Ngai. The Communists attacked ferociously; but half of them were armed with only spears and knives. After the battle, U.S. troops picked up twenty spears, thirty-five knives, and one rifle that had been left behind.

---

102 True or false: A Vietcong assault team entered the U.S. Embassy in Saigon during the Tet Offensive.

ANS: False. The Vietcong sapper squad only made it as far as the Embassy grounds.

103 What strategically important city in north-central Vietnam was held by the Communists for twenty-five days after the Tet Offensive began?

ANS: Hue.

104 What historical landmark in Hue was desperately sought by the Communists and, once they had it, by the United States and the ARVN?

ANS: The thirteenth-century citadel that was the center of the old imperial capital.

105 True or false: The battle for Hue involved the heaviest concentration of forces on both sides to date.

ANS: True. On the Communist side were two NVA regiments and two Vietcong sapper battalions. They faced a combination of eight U.S. and thirteen ARVN infantry battalions.

106 How long did the Communist flag fly over Hue?

ANS: Thirty days.

107 What grisly discovery was made in the fields across from Hue after the battle?

ANS: Mass graves. Perhaps 2,800 residents had been slaughtered by the Communists.

108 What strategically important aspect of the ARVN's military conduct did U.S. advisers discover during Tet?

ANS: They had been almost completely infiltrated by Communist agents.

109 The Tet Offensive and the battle of Khe Sanh moved LBJ to call a meeting of the "wise men." Who were they?

ANS: Formally known as the Senior Advisory Group on Vietnam, the group of fifteen establishment diplomatic and military figures had been formed by LBJ in early 1966 to consult with him on the war. It included Dean Acheson, Gen. Omar Bradley, George Ball, Clark Clifford, and Henry Cabot Lodge, among others.

110 What was the main lesson that the "wise men" drew from its questioning of U.S. officials on their war strategy?

ANS: That the war could not be won.

111 Who won the battle of Tet?

ANS: Although the Communists were routed militarily and suffered massive casualties, the early verdict of history was that they had scored a decisive, strategic victory. The American people had lost confidence in the rosy predictions of the Johnson Administration and now concluded that the war would have to continue for many years.

112 During the week of February 10–17, 1968, 543 Americans were killed in action and 2,547 were wounded. Why is this significant?

ANS: It was the highest weekly casualty total of the war.

113 What did General Westmoreland want from LBJ ten days later?

ANS: An additional 206,000 troops.

114 On March 1, 1968, who replaced Robert S. McNamara as U.S. secretary of defense?
   a) Chester Bowles
   b) George Ball
   c) Clark Clifford
   d) Christian Herter
   e) Cyrus Vance

ANS: c.

115 In terms of the U.S. role in Vietnam, what was significant about the year 1968?

ANS: It was the year of the most dramatic increase in the number of U.S. casualties in South Vietnam; it nearly doubled the total from all the previous years combined (16,021) to 30,610. In 1968 alone, 14,589 were killed.

116 By 1969, the rising toll of U.S. casualties had become a political liability. The newly elected Nixon Administration decided to shift the burden of frontline fighting to the ARVN. What was this strategy labeled?

ANS: "Vietnamization."

117   Who was Nixon's secretary of defense?

ANS: Melvin Laird.

118   "Vietnamization" may have put too much of a burden on the Saigon troops, whose main problem was
   a) malnutrition
   b) lack of military supplies
   c) desertion
   d) lack of mobility

ANS: C.

119   True or false: The number of desertions from the Saigon ranks in 1969 alone topped 100,000.

ANS: True. It was 107,000.

120   What was the main effect of "Vietnamization" on U.S. troops?
   a) shattered morale
   b) reluctance to engage in combat
   c) increased drug use
   d) breakdown of unit discipline
   e) corruption of officer corps

ANS: All of the above.

121   The Big Red One was the nickname of the First Infantry Division. After years of heavy casualties and sinking morale in Vietnam, what did draftees begin calling it?

ANS: The Big *Dead* One.

122　In January 1969, the Ninth Marines launched one of the biggest operations of the war against NVA main force units near the Laotian border. This resulted in awesome casualties on both sides and one of largest losses of Communist weapons and equipment up to that time. The operation was called
　a) Arizona Flats
　b) Ranch Hand
　c) Dewey Canyon
　d) Boxcar
　e) Rockpile

ANS: c.

123　On April 30, 1969, the number of U.S. troops in South Vietnam reached its peak. What was it?
　a) 536,100
　b) 543,400
　c) 577,600
　d) 599,900
　e) 600,000

ANS: b.

124　Although big battles were supposedly no longer the hallmark of U.S. strategy in Vietnam, U.S. Marines, U.S. Army units, and ARVN troops engaged the NVA in a ferocious fight at Ap Bia Hill in May 1969. What nickname did GIs give it that instantly became gruesomely memorable?

ANS: Hamburger Hill.

125　Soon after news of the appalling U.S. casualty rate at Hamburger Hill reached stateside, some disgruntled GIs began offering $10,000 rewards for the assassination of officers ordering similar attacks. The assassinations, when carried out, earned another GI nickname. What was it?

ANS: "Fragging," from rolling fragmentation grenades under the tent flaps of targeted officers.

126 Fragging received a lot of stateside press in 1969. How many officers and NCOs in the U.S. Army alone were officially reported killed by fragging in that year?
   a) 37
   b) 137
   c) 237
   d) 370

ANS: a.

127 Less than a week after the mayhem at Hamburger Hill, *Life* magazine published a shocking and memorable pictorial spread dealing with the war. What was its most remembered aspect?

ANS: The individual pictures of 241 dead GIs that began on the cover.

128 What was the White House response to the death toll and publicity?
   a) to send more troops
   b) to send less troops
   c) to conduct more air raids
   d) scale back U.S. ground attacks

ANS: d.

129 On June 8, 1969, President Nixon made what announcement that changed the course of the Vietnam War?

ANS: The beginning of U.S. withdrawals from Vietnam.

130 How many troops were to be withdrawn in the first increment?

ANS: 25,000.

131 What was the first unit to be withdrawn, and when?

ANS: All but the Third Brigade of the Ninth Infantry Division, on August 27, 1969.

132 The Ninth Division had seen heavy action in World War II. It participated in the North Africa campaign, Sicily, and the Normandy invasion. It was the first unit to penetrate the Siegfried Line and enter the German homeland. How did its casualties in World War II compare with those it incurred in Vietnam?
   a) about the same
   b) much less
   c) much more

ANS: a. The division suffered more than 20,000 killed or wounded in Vietnam, compared with nearly 23,000 in World War II.

133 It was the first U.S. Marine unit to land in Vietnam in 1965, and it was the first to leave in November 1969. What was it?

ANS: The Third Marine Division.

134 Those Marines thought they were home safely. But major events in 1975 required their emergency return to southeast Asia. What were these events?

a) the evacuation of Phnom Penh
b) the evacuation of Da Nang
c) the evacuation of Saigon
d) the "rescue" of the U.S. ship *Mayaguez*
e) boat people riots in California

ANS: a, b, c, d.

135 A major leadership crisis faced the North Vietnamese on September 3, 1969. What happened?

ANS: Ho Chi Minh died.

136 Nearly 20,000 Vietcong underground political operatives, agents, and tax collectors were "neutralized" by this CIA program in 1969 alone. What was it called?

ANS: Operation Phoenix (in Vietnamese, Phuong Hoang).

137 9,414 Americans were ———— in Vietnam in 1969.
a) captured
b) killed
c) missing in action
d) wounded

ANS: b.

138 By the end of 1969, about how many GIs had been killed in the Vietnam War?
a) 28,000
b) 38,000
c) 40,000
d) 45,000
e) 50,000

ANS: c.

139 On April 29, 1970, even as the United States pursued its withdrawal from Vietnam, one of the biggest and most aggressive combined U.S. and South Vietnamese ground actions of the war was being launched. What was it?

ANS: The invasion of Cambodia.

140 Nixon used a word that later became mockingly famous to describe this invasion. It was
   a) inversion
   b) intervention
   c) incision
   d) incursion
   e) indictment

ANS: d.

141 What was the objective of the "incursion"?

ANS: To destroy North Vietnamese staging grounds inside Cambodia and to buy more time for "Vietnamization."

142 How many miles did the invasion into Cambodia go?
   a) 5
   b) 10
   c) 20
   d) 50
   e) 100

ANS: c.

143 The target area of the Cambodian invasion was known as
   a) Horse's Mouth
   b) Tail of the Donkey
   c) Tuna of the Sea

d) The Worm
e) Fish Hook

ANS: e.

FACT

Historians of the war give mixed grades to the Cambodian "incursion." U.S. and ARVN troops captured huge amounts of Communist war materiel, which may have lessened NVA/VC pressure on Saigon and bought "Vietnamization" another year to work. On the other hand, the Allies failed to destroy any of the rapidly fleeing Communist units. In addition, the United States still bore the brunt of the fighting as ARVN leadership proved once again to be weak and dependent on the Americans, thus providing continuing lack of self-confidence, a factor that would be disastrous in 1975. Finally, the invasion sparked a renewal of rebellion on U.S. campuses, the wholesale resignation of scores of U.S. government officials, and the recruitment of "the White House plumbers."

144 Except for the Cambodian invasion, there were virtually no large, United States–led operations in Vietnam in 1970. The rate of casualties therefore dropped dramatically from that of 1969. How many GIs were killed in 1970?
   a) 3,000
   b) 4,200
   c) 5,200
   d) 6,400
   e) 7,200

ANS: b.

145 On the last day of 1970, the U.S. Navy played its "Vietnamization" card. What did it do?

ANS: The Navy turned over its in-country combat role to its South Vietnamese counterpart.

146 The year 1971 opened with one of the last large-scale U.S. military operations. It was conducted near the site of a previous and similar battle on the Laotian border in Vietnam and was named
  a) Encore
  b) Pegasus II
  c) Dewey Canyon II

ANS: c.

147 A few months later, on February 8, 1971, South Vietnamese troops launched another large-scale cross-border operation with U.S. support called Lam Son 719. Where was this?

ANS: Laos.

148 Who won?

ANS: After early advances, the South Vietnamese troops suffered a humiliating rout, with nearly 50 percent casualties and a disorderly withdrawal.

149 Nevertheless, on July 9, 1971, U.S. troops relinquished control of the defense of what part of South Vietnam to the ARVN?

ANS: The north, starting at the DMZ.

150 In the Laos invasion, a *Life* magazine photographer who had been covering the war for almost ten years was among four photographers who died when enemy fire brought down their helicopter. What was his name?

ANS: Larry Burrows.

151 On August 25, 1971, the first U.S. ground combat unit to arrive in Vietnam six years earlier went home. Which one was it?

ANS: The 173d Airborne Brigade.

FACT

The 173d was distinguished in battle. The brigade won a Presidential Unit Citation for bravery at Dak To against hardened NVA troops in 1967. Additionally, its members won twelve Congressional Medals of Honor during combat, which took the lives of 1,600 GIs.

152 October 8, 1971, marked the last major U.S. ground combat operation in South Vietnam. It took place on the coastal plain of Thua Thien Province, south of Hue, and its name was
  a) Jefferson Glenn
  b) Glenn Miller
  c) Thomas Jefferson
  d) Jefferson Davis
  e) Glenn Davis

ANS: a.

153 On November 12, 1971, President Nixon announced that 45,000 more troops would be coming home. More important, however, he announced a significant change in the role of U.S. troops in Vietnam. What was it?
  a) U.S. ground forces could take only defensive actions
  b) offensive actions would be taken only by South Vietnamese forces

c) both of the above
d) none of the above

ANS: c.

154 On November 29, 1971, a U.S. Army unit that was notorious for its poor performance was deactivated and disbanded. Which was it?

ANS: The Americal Division.

155 In 1971, the number of Americans killed in action returned to the level of 1965, when combat GIs first entered the war. How many was that?

ANS: 1,381 (as opposed to 1,369 in 1965).

156 Of the nearly 58,000 Americans who died in the Vietnam War, what percentage had been killed by the end of 1971?
   a) 65
   b) 80
   c) 90
   d) 95

ANS: b (45,626).

157 In February 1972, the first contingent of ROKs went home. What was a ROK?

ANS: ROK meant Republic of Korea, i.e., South Korean troops.

158 In March 10, 1972, the last U.S. Army division left Vietnam. It was
   a) the Eighty-second
   b) the 173d

   c) the 199th
   d) the 101st
   e) the Fifth Special Forces

ANS: d.

FACT

The 101st ("Screaming Eagles") Airborne Brigade, first organized in World War I, suffered twice as many casualties in
Vietnam as it did in World War II under the command of Gen.
Maxwell B. Taylor in such places as the Normandy invasion
and the Battle of the Bulge. The 101st ended the war with
the capture of Adolf Hitler's mountain redoubt at Berchtes-
gaden. For most of the Vietnam War, it was given the tough
responsibility of blocking NVA infiltration routes out of the
Ashau Valley, suffering almost 20,000 killed or wounded during 1965–72.

159 In May 1972, it was a surprise. It was brutal. It was
called the Easter Offensive. What happened?

ANS: Twelve North Vietnamese divisions, four crossing the
DMZ, unleashed broad attacks on Quang Tri in the north, on
Kontum in the Central Highlands, and on An Loc, a coastal
capital sixty-five miles north of Saigon. On May 1 the Communists hoisted their flag over Quang Tri; only a massive U.S. air
campaign forced them out four months later.

160 What significant event in the continuing "Vietnamization" of the war took place in the midst of the Easter Offensive?

ANS: USARV headquarters was closed down.

161 What lesson did both Vietnamese sides draw from the Easter Offensive?

ANS: Saigon could not hold off the Communists without direct U.S. military intervention.

162 In June 1972, the third commander of all U.S. troops replaced Gen. Creighton Abrams. Who was he?
  a) Gen. Loudon Wainwright
  b) Gen. Maxwell Taylor
  c) Gen. Bruce Palmer, Jr.
  d) Gen. Matthew Ridgeway
  e) Gen. Frederick Weyand

ANS: e.

163 On June 9, 1972, John Paul Vann was killed in action. Who was he?

ANS: A legendary U.S. Army counterinsurgency adviser, thought by his many friends in the field—and in the press—to be the United States's top Vietnam expert. The lieutenant colonel was attached to the U.S. Seventh Division.

164 On June 29, 1972, the 1,200 troops of the 196th Light Infantry Brigade left South Vietnam. What was the significance of that?

ANS: Afterward, there were no U.S. combat units left in Vietnam bigger than a battalion.

165 True or false: After the Third Battalion of the Twenty-first Infantry left two months later, there were no U.S. ground combat units remaining in South Vietnam.

ANS: True.

FACT

The history of the 196th Light Infantry Brigade only went back to 1965, when it was formed for duty in the Dominican Republic.

In 1966, however, Pentagon chiefs decided it wasn't needed there and sent it to Vietnam, where General Westmoreland welcomed it as a godsend. It was one of the few U.S. units to arrive en masse as a unit, crossing the Pacific Ocean in two ships. The troops had only three weeks to prepare before leaving; they received their M-16s only then.

---

166 It was perhaps the largest U.S. military supply depot in the world. On November 11, 1972, it was closed down, bringing to an end all direct U.S. Army participation in the Vietnam War. What was its name?

ANS: Long Binh.

167 Long Binh had a famous stockade that GIs had nicknamed what?

ANS: The LBJ, or Long Binh Jail.

168 By the end of 1972, the U.S. troop presence had dwindled to
   a) 15,000
   b) 24,000
   c) 35,000
   d) 75,000
   e) 110,000

ANS: b.

169 How big were the South Vietnamese armed forces at this point? (Hint: The entire population of South Vietnam was 16 million.)

ANS: More than 1 million men and women.

170 True or false: There were only three hundred Americans killed in Vietnam in 1972.

ANS: True.

171 To the relief of college students and Nixon Administration officials alike, what came to a halt in January 27, 1973?

ANS: The draft.

172 During the Vietnam War, 26.8 million men were of draft age. How many were drafted?
   a) 1.1 million
   b) 2.2 million
   c) 3.3 million
   d) 4.4 million
   e) 5.5 million

ANS: b.

173 Of those who did not enter the military, how many were deferred, exempted, or disqualified?
   a) 15.4 million
   b) 17.6 million
   c) 19.8 million
   d) 22.1 million
   e) 25.4 million

ANS: a.

174 What was the date of the signing of the Paris Peace Agreement?

ANS: January 27, 1973.

175 Did the Saigon government sign the agreement?

ANS: Yes.

176 On January 30, 1973, Melvin Laird stepped down as secretary of defense. Who replaced him?

ANS: Eliot L. Richardson.

177 The war came to an official end for U.S. Army personnel on March 28, 1973, when
   a) the Saigon PX was closed
   b) the bar at the Caravelle BOQ was shut down
   c) the last Filipino rock band departed
   d) the awarding of Vietnam service medals and campaign ribbons was terminated

ANS: d.

178 What did the closing of MACV Saigon headquarters on March 29 mark the end of?

ANS: The U.S. combat presence in South Vietnam.

179 On July 2, 1973, what pipe-smoking hardliner replaced Eliot Richardson as secretary of defense?

ANS: James Schlesinger.

180 Who were the only combat-equipped Americans remaining in South Vietnam at the end of 1973?

ANS: The fifty U.S. Marine Embassy guards.

181 On December 13, 1974, NVA units attacked Saigon positions in Phuoc Long Province and then halted. Why?

ANS: To see if the U.S. would send combat troops back to the war.

182 When did all combat operations by U.S.-supported South Vietnamese troops end?
  a) March 29, 1973
  b) December 13, 1974
  c) April 30, 1975

ANS: c.

183 What caused South Vietnam to stop fighting?

ANS: During March–April 1975, South Vietnam's troops were sent into panic and retreat by the combined Vietcong and North Vietnamese forces. Communist tanks and troops captured Saigon on April 30, 1975, ending the war.

6

THE AIR WAR

1 On Election Day 1964, a group was formed in the Johnson White House to plan bombing strategy against North Vietnam. Of the three Kennedy aides listed below, which one was in charge?
   a) Walt Rostow
   b) Robert McNamara
   c) McGeorge Bundy

ANS: c.

2 What position did McGeorge Bundy's brother William hold in the administration?

ANS: Assistant secretary of state for far eastern affairs.

3 What colorful U.S. Air Force general, later to become a vice-presidential candidate, was sometimes called the Genghis Khan of the Air Force?

ANS: Curtis LeMay, SAC commander and member of the Joint Chiefs of Staff during the early 1960s.

4 In January 1962, the U.S. launched Operation Ranch Hand. What was it?

ANS: An Air Force defoliant operation over South Vietnam.

5 On May 21, 1964, what Laotian leader gave permission for U.S. Air Force low-level reconnaissance flights over his country?

ANS: Prince Souvanna Phouma.

6 What famous quote about the air war against North Vietnam is associated with LeMay?

ANS: "We should bomb them back into the Stone Age."

7 In the fall of 1964, LeMay and U.S. Army Gen. Earl Wheeler led their respective teams in desktop wargames to test the efficacy of an air campaign against North Vietnam. The "U.S." team was led by LeMay, and the "Communist" team by Wheeler. Who "won"?

ANS: Wheeler's "Communists."

8 What were Plan 34A raids?

ANS: Secret U.S. air attacks on North Vietnam before the Tonkin Gulf incident of 1964.

9 This U.S. destroyer was reported to have been under attack in the Tonkin Gulf on August 2, 1964.

ANS: USS *Maddox.*

10 A second U.S. ship patrolling in the Tonkin Gulf was

ANS: The USS *Turner Joy.*

11 LBJ went on television to announce air strikes over North Vietnam in retaliation for Communist raids on the U.S. ships. In military terms, what was highly unusual about his announcement?

ANS: The U.S. war planes hadn't yet arrived over their targets at the time of the announcement.

12 The code name for the bombing raid was
   a) Nat Turner
   b) Turnover
   c) Arrowhead
   d) Pierce Arrow

ANS: d.

13 The two aircraft carriers they flew from were
   a) the *Princeton*
   b) the *America*
   c) the *Constellation*
   d) the *Ticonderoga*
   e) the *Mississippi*
   f) the *Missouri*

ANS: c and d.

14 The U.S. aircraft hit four North Vietnamese patrol boats and bombed oil storage depots. The administration described the mission as
   a) "limited in scale"
   b) "just the beginning"
   c) "massive retaliation"
   d) "a stern warning"

ANS: a.

15 True or false: The U.S. planes all returned safely.

ANS: False. Two planes were shot down, and one pilot was taken prisoner.

16 What was the name of this pilot, the first shot down over North Vietnam?

ANS: Edward Alvarez, Jr.

17 In October 1964, the Vietcong attacked a U.S. air base in South Vietnam, destroying six B-52s. Where was the attack?

ANS: Bien Hoa air base.

18 North Vietnam wasn't the only target for U.S. jets in 1964. Where was Operation Barrel Roll targeted?
   a) China
   b) Laos
   c) Cambodia
   d) Cambodia and Laos

ANS: b.

19 Of the following five civilian advisers to LBJ, which was the only one to oppose the bombing campaign in 1964?
   a) McGeorge Bundy
   b) Walt Rostow
   c) Robert McNamara
   d) George Ball
   e) John McNaughton

ANS: d.

20 There was near-unanimity among LBJ's civilian advisers in favoring slow escalation of the air war. Which important government sectors were against it?

ANS: The Joint Chiefs of Staff and the three key U.S. intelligence agencies dealing with Vietnam—the CIA, the DIA, and the State Department's Bureau of Intelligence and Research. All three felt the air war had to have impact heavier and faster if it were to be effective.

21 In February 1965, General LeMay was replaced as Air Force chief of staff. Who succeeded him?

ANS: Gen. John McConnell.

22 On February 7, 1965, Communist guerrillas dramatically attacked a U.S. military compound in the Central Highlands, killing nine advisers and wounding seventy-six more. Where was the base?

ANS: Pleiku.

23 What was the U.S. response?

ANS: Fourteen hours later, forty-nine jets from the U.S. carriers *Coral Sea* and *Hancock* bombed Dong Hoi, North Vietnam.

24 That air operation had a code name. What was it?
  a) Rolling Thunder
  b) Thunder Shot
  c) Bowling Ball
  d) Fireball
  e) Flaming Dart

ANS: e.

25 Only three days later, LBJ ordered Flaming Dart II, another bombing raid over the north. What triggered it?

ANS: Communist guerrillas had blown up a barracks for U.S. personnel in Quinhon, killing twenty-three and wounding twenty-one.

26 True or false: At this point, the United States had not lost any planes over the north.

ANS: False.

27 When Quinhon was attacked again while U.S. jets were over the north, LBJ unleashed the first sustained bombing campaign against North Vietnam. What was its code name?

ANS: Rolling Thunder.

28 Can you remember the date LBJ decided on it and the date it began?

ANS: February 13 and March 2, 1965, respectively.

29 What was the first objective of the bombing campaign?

ANS: To force Hanoi to drop its support for Communists in the south.

30 When that quickly failed, what was the substitute U.S. objective?

ANS: To force Hanoi to negotiate.

FACT

"He was emotionally committed. No Vietnamese was going to push Lyndon Johnson around and torture and kill American boys without being punished." —from *Vietnam: The Valor and the Sorrow,* by Thomas D. Boettcher.

"He would look around him and see in Bob McNamara that it was technologically feasible, in McGeorge Bundy that it was intellectually respectable, and in Dean Rusk that it was historically necessary." —Tom Wicker, *The New York Times.*

31 Operation Steel Tiger was launched against areas of Laos in April 1965. What was its objective?

ANS: To destroy the Ho Chi Minh Trail.

32 What was the Air Force's most effective weapon over the Ho Chi Minh Trail?
   a) the B-52
   b) Agent Orange
   c) the AC-130 gunship the Spooky

ANS: c.

33 What devices helped pilots find nighttime targets on the Ho Chi Minh Trail?

ANS: Electronic sensors on the ground monitored by aircraft circling above and relayed to a targeting center in Thailand.

34 What was the principal attack fighter-bomber flying from aircraft carriers in the South China Sea?
   a) the A-4 Skyhawk
   b) the F-4 Phantom

c) the F-100 Sabrejet

ANS: a.

35 What was the *Kittyhawk?*

ANS: A U.S. aircraft carrier.

36 What was a Caribou?

ANS: The C-7 Caribou was the principal transport plane used in the early days of the war. It was made by deHavilland of Canada.

37 What was the *Oriskany?*

ANS: One of the U.S. aircraft carriers in the South China Sea.

38 Rolling Thunder was geographically limited to what area?

ANS: Below the 20th parallel in North Vietnam.

39 There were five other early target restrictions. Of the following, what target was *not* prohibited?
   a) civilian installations
   b) river dikes
   c) urban Hanoi
   d) the Ho Chi Minh Trail
   e) North Vietnamese MiG bases
   f) North Vietnamese surface-to-air missile sites

ANS: d.

40 What sector of the government controlled U.S. bombing policy?

ANS: The White House.

41 American pilots were first forbidden to attack SAM sites because
   a) it was too dangerous
   b) they might kill a Soviet instructor
   c) the White House insisted the SAMs wouldn't be used

ANS: b and c.

42 True or false: During Rolling Thunder, U.S. pilots were forbidden to shoot at attacking MiGs.

ANS: False.

43 What was LBJ's Christmas present to Hanoi on December 24, 1965?

ANS: A seven-day bombing halt.

44 The seven-day bombing halt was extended to thirty-seven days, during which LBJ sought diplomatic initiatives to come to terms with Hanoi. What was that period called?

ANS: The Peace Offensive.

45 Meanwhile, we were still bombing Laos. True or false?

ANS: True.

FACT _____

Hanoi received $1.6 billion in foreign economic and military aid during the 1964–65 bombing campaign—four times its losses.

_____

46 A month after the Peace Offensive failed, the 460th, the 366th, the Fourteenth, the 315th, and the Thirty-fifth were sent to Vietnam during February, March, and April. What were they?

ANS: Recon, fighter, air commando, and bomber Air Force units.

47 How many U.S. planes were shot down during Rolling Thunder?

ANS: Fifty-five.

48 What was the workhorse of the U.S. fighter fleet over North Vietnam?

ANS: The F-4 Phantom.

49 Why were some bombs "smart"?

ANS: They had TV lenses through which bombardiers could guide them to targets.

50 What was the principal North Vietnamese antiaircraft missile?

ANS: The SA-2.

51 U.S. pilots feared what weapon even more than the SA-2?

ANS: Radar-controlled antiaircraft artillery with a range of 15,000 feet.

52 Thanh Hoa and Paul Doumer refer to the two most important targets in the North. What were they?

ANS: Bridges.

53 The Battle of the Thanh Hoa Bridge is one of the most famous in U.S. Air Force war history. Why?

ANS: All the U.S. tactical air power applied against it during the entire war could not destroy it.

54 Who was Col. Robinson Risner?

ANS: A U.S. pilot and leader of the first Thanh Hoa Bridge strike. He was shot down over North Vietnam on September 16, 1965.

55 In November 1965, the United States beefed up its Vietnam air power by deploying two tactical fighter wings, the third and the twelfth, to Bien Hoa and where else?

ANS: Cam Ranh.

56 When and where was the B-52 first employed as a tactical weapon in South Vietnam?

ANS: At the battle of the Ia Drang Valley, June 1965.

57 In May 1966, Operation Arc Light, begun in South Viet-

nam in June 1965, was extended to North Vietnam for the first
time. What was Operation Arc Light?

ANS: B-52 attacks.

58 In June 1966, LBJ ordered the bombing of oil installations at what two places in North Vietnam?

ANS: Hanoi and Haiphong.

59 What was the tactical North Vietnamese response to the
U.S. bombing of oil storage depots?

ANS: Hanoi ordered oil shipped in fifty-gallon drums, then dis-
persed them over the countryside in small depots.

60 In December 1966, what *New York Times* correspondent
traveled illegally to Hanoi to report on the U.S. air campaign?
   a) Harrison Ford
   b) Benjamin Harrison
   c) Harrison Salisbury

ANS: c.

61 What was the key aspect of Salisbury's reporting on the
bombing targets in Hanoi that contradicted the Johnson Administration?

ANS: That civilian targets were being hit.

62 LBJ's response was that civilian damage was
   a) on purpose
   b) accidental
   c) of little concern to him

ANS: b. At a New Year's Eve press conference, LBJ said that the civilian damage was inadvertent and that he regretted "every single casualty in both North and South Vietnam."

63 In May 1967, U.S. bombers began hitting a power plant where?

ANS: Hanoi.

64 In December 1967, LBJ offered a bombing halt in exchange for what from Hanoi?
a) "immediate acceptance"
b) "unconditional surrender"
c) "positive response"
d) "foreign aid"
e) "peace mission"

ANS: c.

65 True or false: Hanoi said it would agree to peace talks in exchange for a bombing halt and a cease-fire.

ANS: True.

66 By the time of the 1968 Tet Offensive, how many Air Force generals were assigned to South Vietnam?
a) five
b) ten
c) twenty

ANS: b.

67 On March 31, 1968, frustrated by his lack of success in Vietnam and his diminished political fortunes, what did LBJ announce that he would do?

ANS: Not run for reelection.

68 Overshadowed by LBJ's announcement was another bombing restriction, this time to below the 20th parallel. How much of North Vietnam was now denied to U.S. bombers?

ANS: 90 percent.

69 If peace talks failed, LBJ added, what would he do?
   a) resume bombing north of the 20th parallel
   b) send five times as many bombers into North Vietnam
   c) ask for more troops
   d) consider using atomic weapons on Hanoi
   e) destroy hospitals in Hanoi

ANS: a.

70 Despite all the peace signs from Washington, the bombing continued until when?

ANS: October 31, 1968.

71 What relationship did that date have to U.S. politics?

ANS: The Humphrey-Nixon U.S. presidential elections were less than a week away.

72 True or false: North Vietnam never sent its jets to bomb the south.

ANS: True.

73 True or false: During Rolling Thunder, the United States lost less than a hundred aircraft and the same number of pilots.

ANS: False. The United States lost 918 planes and 818 men.

74   Although there was a "bombing halt," what was allowed to continue under LBJ's formulation?

ANS: Reconnaissance flights over the north.

75   But "protective reaction" was permitted to U.S. pilots. What was that?

ANS: Bombing North Vietnamese air defenses when fired upon.

76   A few days after the 1968 presidential election, Operation Commando Hunt was launched with Air Force, Navy, and Marine aircraft. But there was nothing really new about it: their target had been Washington's nemesis for years. What was it?

ANS: The Ho Chi Minh Trail.

77   What was a bullpup?

ANS: A 250-pound guided missile carried by a U.S. jet.

78   What was a Thunderchief?

ANS: An F-105.

79   What was the code name of the area in the Gulf of Tonkin where U.S. aircraft carriers steamed?

ANS: Yankee Station.

80 U.S. jets also flew missions from where else?

ANS: Okinawa, Guam, and Thailand.

81 U.S. pilots called it Thud Ridge. What was it?

ANS: A limestone ridge running north from Hanoi that protected low-flying U.S. Air Force Thunderbird pilots from Communist groundfire.

82 What was the principal North Vietnamese MiG base?

ANS: Phuc Yen.

83 What was a Super Jolly Green?

ANS: The HH-53, a large U.S. rescue helicopter.

84 What was an A-1E?

ANS: The Skyraider, a prop-driven attack aircraft used mostly for close-in ground support.

85 What was a Bird Dog?

ANS: A single-prop Cessna plane flown by forward air controllers.

86 The air forces developed a new bombing technology using laser beams code-named Pave Nail. What was it?

ANS: A bomb followed a laser beam from another plane locked onto the target.

87 Pilot Jeremiah Denton, who later became the first Republican U.S. senator from Alabama since Reconstruction, sent a famous coded message to the United States when he was trotted out for a prisoners' press conference in Hanoi. What was the message, and how did he send it?

ANS: He spelled *torture* by blinking his eyes in Morse code.

88 In March 18, 1969, a secret bombing campaign was begun. What and where was the target?

ANS: Communist troops in Cambodia.

89 What was its code name?
   a) Order
   b) Napkin
   c) Serviette
   d) Menu
   e) Howard Johnson

ANS: d.

90 True or false: The secret B-52 bombings of Cambodia were confined to the border area with South Vietnam.

ANS: True (to within five miles of the border).

91 How long did Menu remain secret?

ANS: Two months, until May 1969, when it was reported by William Beecher in *The New York Times*. (It was not officially acknowledged by the Nixon Administration until 1973.)

92 What was the Nixon Administration's reaction to the leak of the secret bombing?

ANS: Outrage. It formed the "plumbers" unit and began wire-tapping administration officials and journalists.

93 How long did Menu continue?

ANS: Four years, until August 4, 1973.

FACT

Over 16,000 B-52 missions were flown over Cambodia and almost 385,000 tons of bombs were dropped on it during the four years of the Nixon Administration's secret Operation Menu.

94 In August 1969, a new Air Force Chief of Staff, the third since the bombing began, took over. His name?
  a) **Robert Ryan**
  b) **Ryan O'Neill**
  c) **Nolan Ryan**
  d) **John Ryan**

ANS: d.

95 In February 1970, Operation Good Luck began, with the bombing of Pathet Lao positions. Where in Laos were they?

ANS: The Plain of Jars.

96 At this time, an American who had been a civilian refugee worker in Laos came home and displayed evidence of antipersonnel bombs being dropped on villages. Who was he?

ANS: Fred Branfman.

97 Air operations code-named Patio and Freedom Deal were launched in April–May 1970 in support of what new US/ARVN military initiative?

    a) the invasion of Laos
    b) the invasion of Cambodia
    c) the invasion of Thailand
    d) the invasion of China
    e) secret recon in the Ashau Valley

ANS: b.

98 A U.S. special action team landed in North Vietnam looking for POWs on November 21, 1970. Where did they land, and what happened?

ANS: They landed at Son Tay and discovered that the POWs had been removed months earlier.

99 The leader of the Son Tay mission was a tough, experienced colonel by the name of

    a) Bo Gritz
    b) Chargin' Charlie Beckworth
    c) Arthur D. "Bull" Simons
    d) Bo Diddley
    e) Barry Sadler

ANS: c.

100 At the time of the November 20, 1970, Son Tay raid, what else was the United States doing in North Vietnam?

ANS: Bombing it.

101 Why? Rolling Thunder had ended.

ANS: In retaliation for the shooting down of an Air Force reconnaissance plane.

102 B-52 Arc Light strikes played a crucial role in the dramatic new ground operation launched by ARVN forces on February 8, 1971. What was it?

ANS: Lam Son 719, the invasion of the Ho Chi Minh Trail in Laos.

103 Nixon gave the North Vietnamese a Christmas present in December 1971. What was it?

ANS: A bombing halt.

104 What resumed once more on the day after Christmas 1971?

ANS: The bombing.

105 But what in North Vietnam had *not* been bombed since 1968?

ANS: Hanoi.

106 In March 1972, North Vietnamese divisions swept across the DMZ. What did Nixon do in North Vietnam?

ANS: He resumed the bombing of Hanoi and Haiphong in Operation Linebacker.

107 In May 1972, even as Soviet leaders toasted him in Moscow, President Nixon ordered a dramatic new element in the North Vietnam campaign. What was it?

ANS: Mining of Haiphong Harbor.

108 In the fall of 1972, Gen. John D. Lavelle was called before a congressional committee to explain U.S. bombing policies. Why?

ANS: *The New York Times* had reported that General Lavelle had ordered some twenty-eight bombing missions against North Vietnam, between November 1971 and March 1972, under the guise of "protective reactive" strikes.

109 What happened to him?

ANS: He was stripped of his command, reduced in rank, and cashiered from the Air Force.

110 Operation Linebacker quickly led to new negotiations in Paris, which eventually bogged down again. In response, what military action did Nixon take on December 1972?

ANS: The renewed bombing of Hanoi and Haiphong in Operation Linebacker II.

111 This new bombing of Hanoi and Haiphong instantly became known by a far more critical moniker that mocked the spirit of the season. What was it?

ANS: The Christmas Bombing.

112 What was the famous reported hospital bombed at the time?

ANS: Bach Mai Hospital in Hanoi.

113 When did Hanoi and the United States sign a peace agreement?

ANS: On January 23, 1973.

114 But when did the bombing in Laos end?

ANS: On February 21, 1973.

115 And Cambodia?

ANS: Congress ordered that the bombing stop on August 14, 1973.

116 True or false: U.S. and North Vietnamese losses were about even in air-to-air combat.

ANS: False. The United States lost 92 planes; the North Vietnamese lost 193.

117 How many planes did the U.S. Air Force lose in the war?
   a) 2,257
   b) 3,257
   c) 4,657

ANS: a.

118 How many crewmember casualties did the Air Force suffer in the war?

ANS: 2,218 killed and 3,460 wounded.

119 How many MiGs did U.S. pilots down in the whole war?
   a) 7
   b) 14
   c) 48
   d) 116

ANS: d.

120 How many B-52s were downed over North Vietnam between June 1965 and August 1973?
   a) 12
   b) 29
   c) 35
   d) 47
   e) 75

ANS: b. Seventeen were shot down by hostile fire; twelve crashed "from operational causes."

7

THE WAR AT HOME

1 In the fall of 1963, President Kennedy tried to persuade the publisher of *The New York Times* to remove a reporter who was critical of the war effort from Saigon. Who was this reporter, who later went on to great fame?

ANS: David Halberstam.

2 What American university gained notoriety for training South Vietnam's police force in the 1960s?
  a) University of California
  b) Harvard
  c) Michigan State University
  d) University of Michigan

ANS: c.

3 Saigon's police were nicknamed
  a) the black cats
  b) the yellow menace
  c) the white mice

ANS: c.

4 Complete this slogan, chanted for the first time by antiwar demonstrators at a rally in Washington, D.C., in November 1965:

"Hey! Hey! LBJ! How many ———?"

ANS: kids did you kill today

5 This modest political newsletter, which was written, edited, and produced by a single Washington journalist, became one of the most influential of publications critical of the Vietnam War. What was it?

ANS: *I.F. Stone's Weekly.*

6 What was "the Boston Tea Party of the student revolution"?

ANS: Demonstrations at the University of California, Berkeley, in 1964, which kicked off the Free Speech Movement.

7 Who was Mario Savio?

ANS: The leader of the Free Speech Movement.

8 What does SDS stand for?

ANS: Students for a Democratic Society.

9 By what name was SDS's founding declaration of principles known, after the university town where it was drawn up?
   a) the Port Washington Statement
   b) the Port Huron Statement
   c) the Puerto Rico Statement

ANS: b.

10 Who were, in Norman Mailer's words, the "armies of the night"?

ANS: Antiwar demonstrators converging on Washington, D.C., in October, 1967.

11 What thirty-two-year-old Quaker, in a grisly Vietnam War protest, doused himself with gasoline and fatally set himself on fire outside the Pentagon in 1965?
  a) Morris Ruben
  b) Daniel Ellsberg
  c) Norman Morrison
  d) Norman Harrison

ANS: c.

12 What top Johnson Administration official looked on as Morrison killed himself?

ANS: Secretary of Defense Robert McNamara watched from his office window.

13 In October 1967, five Americans signed a widely published antiwar document, *A Call to Resist Illegitimate Authority*. It later became the basis for the government's use of criminal statutes to prosecute acts of civil disobedience. Name the five signatories from the list below.
  a) Marcus Raskin
  b) Dr. Benjamin Spock
  c) Tom Hayden
  d) Michael Ferber
  e) Rev. William Sloan Coffin
  f) Bobby Seale
  g) Mitchell Goodman

ANS: a, b, d, e, g.

14 What does the word *Cointelpro* mean? What was it about?

ANS: *Cointelpro* stands for "counterintelligence program." It was the acronym for the FBI's surveillance and disruption program against the civil rights and antiwar movements.

15 What was Operation Chaos?

ANS: Similar to the FBI's Cointelpro, it was the CIA's program against the antiwar movement.

16 What Justice Department attorney in particular traveled the country coordinating the prosecution of antiwar figures?

ANS: Guy Goodman.

17 The Black Panthers initially received a great deal of positive publicity for doing what?

ANS: Giving hot breakfasts to ghetto schoolkids.

18 What former leader of the Black Panthers once ran for Mayor of Oakland, California?

ANS: Bobby Seale.

19 Who said, "None of them/No Vietcong ever called me nigger"?

ANS: Cassius Clay (now known as Muhammed Ali).

20 What happened to him then?

ANS: He was stripped of his heavyweight championship title by the World Boxing Authority (WBA).

21 What Black Panther, who was later convicted of rape, eventually joined the Moonies?

ANS: Eldridge Cleaver.

22 What black graduate of Boston University won the Nobel Peace Prize in 1964?

ANS: Dr. Martin Luther King, Jr.

23 At the Riverside Church in New York City on April 4, 1967, Rev. Martin Luther King, Jr., made perhaps his most controversial speech. What was it about?

ANS: In his "Declaration of Independence from the War in Vietnam" King declared that equality for blacks would be set back by the war.

24 Name the Chicago Seven.

ANS: Dave Dellinger, Tom Hayden, Bobby Seale, Rennie Davis, Abbie Hoffman, John Freunds, and Lee Weiner.

25 Who was the judge that presided over the Chicago Seven trial?

ANS: Julius Hoffman.

26 How many U.S. "incidents of desertion" were there, according to the Pentagon, between 1966 and 1973?

ANS: 503,926.

27 How many deserters were still "at large" at the time of President Ford's pardon in 1974?
  a) 28,661
  b) 42,568
  c) 7,114

ANS: a.

28 Who leaked the Pentagon Papers, to what reporter, of what newspaper?
  a) Daniel Ellsberg, to Bob Woodward of *The Washington Post.*
  b) George Ball, to Carl Bernstein of *The Washington Post.*
  c) Daniel Ellsberg, to Neil Sheehan of *The New York Times.*
  d) Robert McNamara, to Robert Healy of *The Boston Globe.*

ANS: c.

29 Who was Daniel Ellsberg's psychiatrist, and why was he famous in the Nixon era?

ANS: Dr. Lewis Fielding's office was broken into by the Watergate burglars.

FACT

Long before he became famous—or infamous—as the source of the Pentagon Papers leak, Daniel Ellsberg had been a highly respected former Marine officer and so-called "defense intellectual." According to an account by David Halberstam in *The Best and the Brightest,* President-elect John F. Kennedy got the idea to emphasize "the infantryman" as the central thrust of his new military policy from Ellsberg.

---

30 When the tiny village of Ben Tre in South Vietnam was totally destroyed by U.S. airpower during the Tet attacks, what remark by an unidentified U.S. major in the February 6, 1968, *New York Times* summed up the futility of the war for many?

ANS: "It became necessary to destroy the town to save it."

31 What brothers became famous for their antiwar activities?
   a) the Hayden brothers
   b) the Berrigan brothers
   c) the Blues brothers
   d) the Smothers brothers
   e) the Kennedy brothers

ANS: b.

32 "Be clean for ———" was a slogan in the 1968 Democratic primary campaign. Can you complete the slogan? Whose slogan was it?

ANS: Gene, who was Sen. Eugene McCarthy.

33 What did that slogan mean?

ANS: It urged young volunteers on the McCarthy campaign to cut their hair before ringing doorbells, so as not to offend "straight" people by a sloppy appearance.

34   In March 1968 occurred four major domestic U.S. political events revolving around the war. Out of the following six, what were they?

a) On March 12, dark-horse candidate Eugene McCarthy came within a handful of votes of defeating President Johnson in the New Hampshire primary.

b) On March 16, Robert Kennedy announced his presidential candidacy.

c) On March 22, Johnson announced that he had relieved Gen. William Westmoreland of his command.

d) On March 24, Alabama Governor George Wallace was slain.

e) On March 26, Rep. Paul "Pete" McCloskey announced that he would challenge Richard Nixon in the primaries.

f) On March 31, Johnson announced that he would not run for reelection.

ANS: a, b, c, and f.

35   Who made up the Peace and Freedom presidential ticket in 1968?

ANS: Shirley Chisholm and Benjamin Spock.

36   Spiro Agnew denounced television commentators as what?

ANS: "Nattering nabobs of negativism."

37   What was the Committee of Concerned Asian Scholars?

ANS: A national organization of graduate students and professors opposed to the war.

38 What present-day U.S. senator appeared before the Senate Foreign Relations Committee as an ex-GI to plead, "Who could ask a man to be the last man to die in Vietnam?"

ANS: John F. Kerry of Massachusetts, who led Vietnam Veterans Against the War.

39 What was the Winter Soldier Investigation?

ANS: The public testimony of U.S. soldiers about their actions in Vietnam, sponsored by the Vietnam Veterans Against the War, first in Detroit, later in Boston.

40 The Cooper-Church Amendment became effective December 29, 1969. Who was Cooper, and who was Church?

ANS: John Sherman Cooper was a U.S. senator from Kentucky; Frank Church was a U.S. senator from Idaho.

41 Their legislation prohibited U.S. ground troops from entering
   a) Laos and Thailand
   b) Laos and Cambodia
   c) Laos, Cambodia, and Thailand

ANS: a.

42 The accidental B-52 bombing of what "friendly" Cambodian village on August 6, 1973, enraged the U.S. public?
   a) Kampong Cham
   b) Neak Luong
   c) Son My

ANS: b.

43   Dewey Canyon I was the covert invasion of Laos in 1969. Dewey Canyon II was the overt invasion of Laos in February 1971. What was Dewey Canyon III (which didn't even take place in Asia)?

ANS: The demonstration of Vietnam Veterans Against the War in Washington in April 1971.

44   How many students were killed at Kent State?

ANS: Four.

45   On March 13, 1970, aboard the U.S. cargo ship *Columbia Eagle* in the Gulf of Siam, one of the most unusual incidents in the annals of antiVietnam War events occurred. What happened?

ANS: Two crewmen pulled a gun on the captain, commandeered the ship, which was full of bombs for B-52s in Thailand, and changed its course.

FACT

Merchant Marines Clyde McKay and Alvin Glatowski had seemed apolitical before the takeover of the S.S. *Columbia Eagle,* according to fellow crewmembers. They didn't know what to do after their mutiny and finally ordered the captain to anchor off Cambodia, which a few days earlier had experienced the coup that expelled Prince Sihanouk and brought Lon Nol and his generals to power. Both McKay and Glatowski made their way to shore, where they were eventually arrested by Lon Nol. McKay escaped and was last seen heading toward Communist troops near Siem Reap; Glatowski turned himself in to the U.S. Embassy and returned home for trial and sentencing. He was paroled from the federal prison at Lompoc, California, after five years in 1977.

46 The spring of 1969 saw some of the greatest confrontations ever between students and authorities. One of the biggest battles was fought over a small piece of real estate in Berkeley, California, where eight hundred were arrested, thirty wounded, and one killed. It was called
   a) Sproul Plaza
   b) People's Park
   c) Telegraph Avenue

ANS: b.

47 "These students are going to have to find out what law and order are all about," the commander of the Ohio National Guard at Kent State told reporters before moving in on protesters. His name was
   a) Brig. Gen. Robert Westminster
   b) Brig. Gen. Robert Canterbury
   c) Brig. Gen. Ralph Cranmore

ANS: b.

48 How many colleges closed down for the rest of the year as a direct result of the April 1970 Cambodian invasion and the Kent State shootings?

ANS: 286.

49 The shootings at Kent State are well known. But where had police killed two students and wounded nine more with buckshot only a few weeks earlier?

ANS: Jackson State College, Mississippi.

50 In President Nixon's words, who was "silent" in the battle for public opinion?

ANS: The "majority" of Americans, who he said supported the war.

51 President Nixon called his plan to end the war
   a) "silent"
   b) "secret"
   c) "complicated"

ANS: b.

52 Vice President Spiro Agnew was sent around the United States making alliterative allegations that condemned students and other war critics. Fill in the blanks of this description dissidents:
"An effete corps of ——— snobs who characterize themselves as ———."

ANS: impudent; intellectuals

53 In early 1968, Columbia students occupied and held the office of the university's president. He was
   a) Clark Kerr
   b) Nathan Pusey
   c) Grayson Kirk

ANS: c.

54 Woodstock, the biggest counterculture event of the decade, was held on a farm in upstate New York. Who owned the farm?
   a) Les Baxter
   b) Axel Yazdel
   c) Max Yasgur

ANS: c.

55 At the time of Woodstock, at what percent did Nixon's public approval rating stand?
   a) 23
   b) 49
   c) 68

ANS: c.

56 What was bombed at the University of Wisconsin, resulting in the death of a physicist, the injury of four others, and $6 million worth of damage?

ANS: The Army Mathematics Research Center.

57 Who did it?

ANS: John Sinclair.

Numbers on trial: How many people were tried for acts of antiwar activity in each of the following cities?
58   Chicago
59   Harrisburg
60   Camden
61   Seattle
62   Kansas City
63   Evanston
64   Gainesville

ANS: 58-seven, 59-seven, 60-seventeen, 61-seven, 62-four, 63-four, 64-eight.

65 The May 2 Movement, an offshoot of the Progressive Labor Party, was an early opponent of the war. What relatively mild action taken by that group in late May 1964 caused a wide reaction?

ANS: It took out an ad in *The New York Herald Tribune* denouncing the war and listing the names of 14,339 men of draft age who pledged not fight in Vietnam.

66 What was SNCC?

ANS: The Student Nonviolent Coordinating Committee, a civil rights group formed in April 1960, made up mostly of black college students.

67 SNCC, usually pronounced *"snick,"* became active in the antiwar movement under what charismatic, militant leader?
   a) H. Rap Brown
   b) Ralph Abernathy
   c) Eldridge Cleaver
   d) Bobby Seale
   e) Stokely Carmichael

ANS: e.

68 In 1964 Carmichael uttered a notorious phrase that enraged feminists. He averred that "the only position for women in SNCC is ———."

ANS: prone.

69 What was the leading antiwar magazine of the 1960s, the only one of its kind ever to reach a mass audience by melding slick graphics and antiwar politics and promoting a counterculture life-style?
   a) *The Nation*
   b) *The Masses*
   c) *Ramparts*
   d) *The Progressive*
   e) *I.F. Stone's Weekly*

ANS: C.

70 In May 1967, this leading civil rights leader's speech, a "Declaration of Independence from the War in Vietnam," was reprinted as a magazine article and had a great influence in the antiwar movement. Who was the author and where was it published?

ANS: Rev. Martin Luther King, Jr.; *Ramparts Magazine.*

71 What were teach-ins?

ANS: Demonstrations held at colleges and universities in the mid-1960s in which students, professors, and others spoke out against U.S. involvement in Vietnam.

72 Where and when was the first teach-in?

ANS: At the University of Michigan at Ann Arbor, on March 24, 1965.

73 What "national teach-in" took place over the course of three weeks in January and February 1966 and was led by Senator J. William Fulbright?

ANS: It was a series of nationally televised hearings held by the U.S. Senate Foreign Relations Committee, examining the U.S. role in Vietnam.

74 In the spring of 1966, the Big Lake One incident took place in Minnesota. What was it, and why was it important?

ANS: Barry Bondhus, who was eligible for the draft, broke into his hometown draft board's headquarters and smeared human feces over dozens of records. It was the first draft-board trashing protest; scores more took place across the country in the following years.

75 Three U.S. soldiers—Pvt. Dennis Mora, PFC James Johnson, and Pvt. David Samas—made a public statement in 1966 that they would refuse to go to Vietnam. The three were court-martialed and spent two years in prison. They became known as
   a) the Fort Worth Three
   b) the DMZs
   c) the Port Huron Three
   d) the Fort Hood Three
   e) the Chicago Three

ANS: d.

76 As far back as the 1950s, important, high-level military voices argued that we should not get involved in Indochina. One was President Eisenhower's personal representative to Saigon, Gen. J. Lawton Collins. What was his nickname?

ANS: "Lightnin' Joe" Collins.

77 Name seven U.S. senators who spoke out loudly against the war *before* the 1965 escalation.

ANS: Frank Church, John Sherman Cooper, George McGovern, Gaylord Nelson, J. William Fulbright, Ernest Gruening, and Wayne Morse.

78 What do these eight U.S. names have in common: Norman Morrison, Roger LaPorte, Hiroko Hayaski, Florence Beaumont, Erik Thoen, Ronald Brazee, George Winney, Alice Herz?

ANS: They all burned themselves to death in personal protests against U.S. involvement in the Vietnam War.

79   Who was Bertrand Russell?

ANS: A British philosopher and mathematician who organized 1967 "war crime trials" regarding U.S. behavior in Vietnam.

80   This superb long-distance runner and tournament-level golfer graduated Phi Beta Kappa from Yale and attended Oxford on a fellowship. He spent three years in federal prisons for refusing to register for the draft in World War II, and years later he became one of the Chicago Seven. Who was he?
 a) Tom Hayden
 b) Bobby Seale
 c) Abe Peck
 d) Dave Dellinger
 e) Rennie Davis

ANS: d.

81   What year did Dellinger make his first speech against U.S. involvement in Vietnam?

ANS: In April 1963, in the Easter Peace Walk in New York City.

82   President Johnson considered this television news anchor's decision to declare the war a "stalemate" after Tet a serious blow. Who said it, adding that the United States was "bogged down" in Vietnam?

ANS: Walter Cronkite.

83   In what year did U.S. public opinion polls for the first time show that the majority of Americans thought it was wrong to be in Vietnam?

ANS: 1967.

84 Who was called "Hanoi Jane" by her detractors because of her visits to North Vietnam during the war and her outspokenness against U.S. involvement?

ANS: Jane Fonda.

85 Canada was the most popular destinations for American men who went into exile abroad rather than serve in the U.S. Army. What was the second favorite?

ANS: Sweden.

86 In August 1964, the U.S. House of Representatives debated the Johnson Administration's Tonkin Gulf resolution. After forty minutes, did they favor it or deplore it?

ANS: They favored it.

87 What was the vote?

ANS: 416 to 0, with New York's Rep. Adam Clayton Powell voting "present."

88 What is SANE?

ANS: The Committee for a Sane Nuclear Policy.

89 What leading antiwar protestor was also well known as a baby doctor?

ANS: Benjamin Spock.

90   Who was Norman Thomas?

ANS: Perennial candidate for president on the Socialist ticket.

91   November 27, 1965, was the date of the first Washington demonstration organized specifically against the war in Vietnam. How many people attended?
   a) 10,000
   b) 25,000
   c) 40,000
   d) 65,000
   e) 100,000

ANS: b.

92   In a May 17, 1966, speech what did President Johnson term those who protested the war, and where did he say this?
   a) "nattering nabobs of negativism"
   b) "nervous nellies"
   c) "cowards"
   d) "sunshine patriots"
   e) "winter soldiers"
   f) all of the above

ANS: b, at a Cook County Democratic dinner in Chicago.

93   He was called "the Gandhi of the antiwar movement." What leading, early opponent of the war visited Hanoi as a radical cleric and died on February 11, 1967?

ANS: Rev. A.J. Muste.

94   In February 1967 a group of 2,500 members of what women's peace group marched on the Pentagon and presented their demand that the United States get out of Vietnam?

ANS: Women's Strike for Peace.

95 Dow Chemical was the target of many antiwar protests, especially by students at college campuses when the company's representatives came recruiting. Why?

ANS: It was the only company that manufactured napalm.

96 What was the most spectacular anti-Dow demonstration?

ANS: It took place on March 22, 1969, when nine radical Catholics, most of them priests, broke into Dow's Washington, D.C., offices, tore the place apart, destroyed files, and doused the office with blood.

97 When was the first mass draft card burning?

ANS: On April 15, 1967, at the Spring Mobilization to End the War march in New York City. In Central Park before the march began, about seventy men put the torch to their draft cards. Several women, holding half of their husbands' or boyfriends' cards, joined them.

98 He came from a blue-blood family in Virginia. His father was a member of President Truman's Council of Economic Advisers and later became secretary of labor. He was one of the most active antiwar protestors and a member of the Chicago 7. Who was he?

ANS: Rennie Davis.

99 What Argentine doctor became a heroic symbol of Third World revolution for young Americans?

ANS: Ernesto "Che" Guevara.

100   Where and when did he die?

ANS: On October 7, 1967, Che was killed by a Bolivian counter-insurgency team, assisted by the CIA.

101   True or false: Eugene McCarthy won the New Hampshire Democratic presidential primary in 1968.

ANS: False. McCarthy won 40 percent of the vote.

102   True or false: On the night Robert F. Kennedy was assassinated, he had just triumphed over McCarthy in the California primary by 46 percent to 41 percent.

ANS: True.

103   In Chicago in 1968, what did the crowd chant outside the Democratic National Convention as police beat them in full view of the press and television cameras?
   a) "Joy to the world"
   b) "The whole world's a stage"
   c) "We are the world"
   d) "The whole world is watching"

ANS: d.

104   True or false: Except for Chicago during the Democratic Convention, there were no antiwar demonstrations of comparable size in 1968 in the United States.

ANS: True.

105   True or false: In mid-October 1968, McGeorge Bundy, a presidential adviser and architect of U.S. Vietnam policy from the days of President Kennedy, changed his mind and publicly called for U.S. withdrawal.

ANS: True.

106 Who was Captain Howard Levy, M.D., and why should we remember his name in an antiwar context?

ANS: This Green Beret captain went on trial for disobedience when he refused to take part in a training program for soldiers on the way to Vietnam in 1967. He was convicted and sent to Leavenworth federal penetentiary.

107 What antiwar group sponsored the Days of Rage in Chicago in 1969?

ANS: SDS, the Students for a Democratic Society, who terrorized an upper-crust Chicago neighborhood, beating up residents, smashing windows and cars, and fighting with police in the hope that it would radicalize America.

108 When was the Moratorium, the high point of the antiwar movement and its greatest success, in which at least 250,000 protestors came together for the largest antiwar gathering in Washington up to that time?

ANS: November 15, 1969.

109 About how many terrorist bombings in the name of ending the war occurred in 1970?
   a) 15
   b) 150
   c) 250
   d) 350
   e) 500

ANS: c, or almost 250, which included 6 deaths and 247 cases of arson.

110 **What happened to Black Panther leader Fred Hampton as he slept in his Chicago bed on December 4, 1969?**

ANS: He was shot and killed by police. Another Panther, Mark Clark, was also killed in the police raid.

111 **True or false: The Chicago police were exonerated from any blame in their deaths.**

ANS: False. A grand jury determined that the police were guilty of murder.

112 **What daughter of a wealthy Michigan family was killed when a bomb accidentally exploded in a Greenwich Village townhouse on March 6, 1970?**
a) Diana Oughton
b) Kathy Wilkerson
c) Kathy Boudin
d) Patty Hearst

ANS: a.

113 **Of what underground antiwar group was she a member?**

ANS: The Weathermen.

114 **Was anyone else killed?**

ANS: Yes, Terry Robbins and Ted Gold. Two who escaped were Kathy Wilkerson, whose father owned the building, and Kathy Boudin.

115 Boudin's father is a well-known New York attorney. Who is her uncle, an equally well-known crusading antiwar journalist?

ANS: I.F. Stone.

116 Who said this about student protesters: "You see these bums, you know, blowin' up the campuses. Listen, the boys that are on the college campuses today are the luckiest people in the world . . . and here they are burnin' up the books, I mean, stormin' around about this issue, I mean, you name it—get rid of the war, there'll be another one."

ANS: President Nixon, walking through the lobby of the Pentagon on May 1, 1970, the day after the Cambodian invasion.

117 Which member of President Nixon's cabinet publicly protested the "bums" remark and disassociated himself from Nixon's war policies?

ANS: Secretary of the Interior Walter J. Hickel. He was fired by Nixon after the November 1970 election.

118 On the night before a large demonstration in Washington to protest the Cambodian invasion, President Nixon made how many telephone calls, according to White House logs, between 9:22 P.M. and 4:22 A.M.?

ANS: Fifty-one, including twenty-six after midnight. Nixon and his valet, Manolo Sanchez, left the White House at about 4:30 A.M. and went to the Lincoln Memorial, where he had a "rap" session with protesters. They reported that the president spoke randomly and aimlessly.

119 True or false: During the May Day demonstrations in Washington in 1971, D.C. police made the largest number of arrests in any demonstration in U.S. history.

ANS: True. About 7,000 people were arrested—so many that police had to pen suspects up in RFK Stadium, the city's football stadium, and the DC Coliseum, a hockey arena.

120   When did *The New York Times* begin publishing the Pentagon Papers?

ANS: Sunday, June 13, 1971.

121   What other papers rapidly followed suit?

ANS: *The Washington Post* and *The Boston Globe.*

122   True or false: Among the charges leveled against the Harrisburg Seven was conspiracy to kidnap Henry Kissinger and to hold him until the United States stopped bombing North Vietnam.

ANS: True.

123   True or false: They were convicted of this charge.

ANS: False.

8

VIETNAM IN BOOKS, MOVIES, AND MUSIC

1 In 1984, what Bruce Springsteen album contained a tune that dealt with the problems of a returning Vietnam veteran?

ANS: *Born in the U.S.A.*

2 *Brothers in Arms* is the title of both a rock album and a book about Vietnam. Name the band and the author.
   a) the Band and Bob Dylan
   b) the Eagles and Dylan Thomas
   c) Dire Straits and William Broyles
   d) Jefferson Starship and James Webb
   e) the Byrds and Alfred Hitchcock

ANS: c.

3 Did *New York Times* reporter David Halberstam ever write a novel about Vietnam?

ANS: Yes—*One Very Hot Day.*

4   What highly acclaimed 1978 nonfiction book, based on reporting by *Esquire*'s correspondent in Vietnam, contained vivid descriptions of the rock and roll music that was so much a part of U.S. soldiers' environment in Vietnam?

ANS: *Dispatches* by Michael Herr.

5   Herr wrote the voice-over narrative in what Vietnam War film, directed by Francis Ford Coppola?

ANS: *Apocalypse Now.*

6   What haunting song by The Doors played over the closing credits in that movie?

ANS: "The End."

7   The character played by Marlon Brando was called Kurtz. He summed up the movie's theme by growling, "The horror, the horror." In what great literary work does the character Kurtz utter those same words?

ANS: Joseph Conrad's *Heart of Darkness.*

8   Who sang this antiwar song's opening line, "When the truth is found to be lies"?

ANS: Grace Slick of the Jefferson Airplane.

9   Name that tune.

ANS: "Somebody to Love."

10 What was the name of Vietnam vet John Del Vecchio's highly praised 1982 Vietnam War novel?

  a) *The 13th Valley*
  b) *The 16th Parallel*
  c) *Fields of Fire*
  d) *Wounds of War*
  e) *The Thin Red Line*

ANS: a.

11 The 1983 bibliography, *Vietnam War Literature* by John Newman, listed how many Vietnam novels, memoirs, and journalistic accounts published between 1965 and 1981?

ANS: 116.

12 By 1984, archivists at Colorado State University had compiled a list of how many Vietnam novels?

ANS: About two hundred.

13 What book by Ronald J. Glasser gives a first-person account of a doctor's year treating the wounded of Vietnam in a burn ward in Japan?

ANS: *365 Days.*

14 True or false: *365 Days* was banned from a high school library because of allegedly obscene language.

ANS: True. The town of Baileyville, Maine, banned the book in 1981.

15 What was the name and author of a 1976 memoir about joining the Marines as a patriotic eighteen-year-old and becoming disillusioned after severe wounds in Vietnam?

ANS: *Born on the Fourth of July* by Ron Kovic.

16 Most top-ten lists of Vietnam War books contain this memoir by Philip Caputo, which later was made into a made-for-TV movie. It tells the story of Caputo's tour in Vietnam with the Marines in 1965, and it ends with a description of the fall of Saigon in 1975, which Caputo covered as a journalist. Name the book, which came out in 1977.

ANS: *A Rumor of War.*

17 *Charlie Company: What Vietnam Did to Us* was a fifty-one-page, 25,000-word special article that appeared at record length on December 14, 1981. It told the story of a group of infantrymen in Vietnam and later was the basis of a CBS News special. What magazine did it appear in, and who wrote it?

ANS: *Newsweek.* The special section was written by Peter Goldman and Tony Fuller.

18 *Chickenhawk,* a memoir about a helicopter pilot's 1965 Vietnam tour by Robert C. Mason, was published under unusual circumstances in 1983. What were they?

ANS: The author was in jail for smuggling drugs.

19 This 1982 critique of what went wrong in Vietnam, written by a U.S. Army staff officer, was published by a small press, is still in print, and in fact is used as a textbook for Vietnam War courses in many colleges and universities. Name the author and the book.

ANS: *On Strategy* by Col. Harry G. Summers, Jr.

20 Summers retired from the Army in 1985. What was his next job?
   a) senior military correspondent for *U.S. News & World Report*
   b) senior adviser to the U.S. Senate Armed Services Committee
   c) senior adviser to the Department of the Army's Planning Division
   d) senior correspondent for ABC News

ANS: a.

21 In *Conversations With the Enemy* (1983), this onetime Marine POW who was tried for desertion after he came home in 1979 told his story to authors Duncan Spencer and Winston Groom. He was the last POW to be released from Vietnam. Who was he?
   a) Robinson Reisner
   b) Jeremiah Denton
   c) Robert Garwood

ANS: c.

22 This 1985 book provided a close look at the rift that broke out after 1975 between the North and South Vietnamese Communists. It tells the story of a Communist who rose to become minister of justice in the Provisional Revolutionary Government before defecting from Ho Chi Minh City in 1978. Name the book and author.

ANS: *A Vietcong Memoir* by Truong Nhu Tang, with David Chanoff and Doan Van Toai.

23 Who wrote *The Vietnamese Gulag,* a 1986 account of disillusionment with the victorious Communists in Vietnam?
a) Doan Van Toai
b) Nguyen Van Thieu
c) Le Duc Tho
d) Nguyen Ai Quoc

ANS: a.

24 What 1969 Robert Altman movie starring Elliott Gould and Donald Sutherland later spawned a very popular TV show? It was set in Korea during the 1950s, but its unstated theme was Vietnam.

ANS: *M*A*S*H.*

25 What actors replaced Gould and Sutherland for the TV series?

ANS: Wayne Rogers and Alan Alda.

26 What TV cop show of the 1970s was notorious for portraying Vietnam veterans as deranged, psychotic killers?
a) Barney Miller
b) Kojak
c) Cagney and Lacey

ANS: b.

27 In what violent film of the early 1970s does a character named Travis Bickle, a haunted Vietnam vet with a shaved head, go on a violent, psychotic rampage? Who played Bickle?

ANS: *Taxi Driver;* Robert DeNiro.

28 In what other Vietnam-oriented film did DeNiro star?

ANS: *The Deer Hunter.*

29 Vietnam vet Tom Bird started what theater group in 1978? It uses Vietnam vets and specializes in plays about Vietnam.

ANS: The Veterans' Ensemble Theater Company.

30 What Broadway hit musical of the late 1960s, later a movie, whose one-word title is drawn from a part of the human anatomy, featured a character who was drafted for the war in Vietnam?

ANS: *Hair.*

31 What controversial Broadway play cruelly lampooned President Johnson during the Vietnam War?

ANS: *MacBird.*

32 From the following list, select three antiwar dramas by playwright David Rabe.
  a) *MacBird*
  b) *The Basic Training of Pavlo Hummel*
  c) *Sticks and Bones*
  d) *Tracers*
  e) *Streamers*

ANS: b, c, and e.

33 What is the significance of the 1979 play *G.R. Point* by David Berry?

ANS: It was the first play set in Vietnam to appear on Broadway.

34 What popular TV show of the early 1980s starred "Mr. T" as one of a group of former Vietnam buddies now fighting criminals back home?

ANS: *The A-Team*.

35 True or false: Tom Selleck is a Vietnam veteran.

ANS: False. He only plays a Vietnam vet as TV's *Magnum, P.I.*

36 Is Sylvester "Rambo" Stallone a Vietnam vet?

ANS: No. He taught at a girls' school in Switzerland during the war.

37 Which of the characters Sonny Crockett and Ricardo Tubbs on *Miami Vice* is a Vietnam vet?

ANS: Crockett.

38 Who immortalized four protestors shot dead by Ohio State National Guard troops at Kent State University in 1970 in the song "Ohio"?

ANS: Neil Young wrote it; Crosby, Stills, Nash, and Young performed it. (In 1984 Young endorsed Ronald Reagan for President.)

39 This Vietnam veteran wrote screenplays for *Midnight Express* and *Salvador* before creating the 1986 Vietnam film epic, *Platoon*. His name?

ANS: Oliver Stone.

40 What other Vietnam-oriented movie won the Oscar for best film in 1978?

ANS: *The Deer Hunter.*

41 In the popular country-pop song of 1967, "Ruby Don't Take Your Love to Town," what was the matter with the veteran of whom Kenny Rogers sang and Mel Tillis wrote?

ANS: His legs were "bent and paralyzed."

42 What song raised draft dodging to an honorable national pastime?

ANS: "Alice's Restaurant."

43 The son sang it; his father was a folk hero before him. Who were they?
   a) Tommy and Jimmy Dorsey
   b) Johnny and Roseann Cash
   c) Hank Williams Jr. and Sr.
   d) Merle and Doc Watson
   e) Woody and Arlo Guthrie

ANS: e.

44 What folk rocker in 1969 sang "To Susie on the west coast waiting, from Andy in Vietnam fighting"?

ANS: Donovan.

45 John Prine wrote and performed what song about a veteran who came home from Vietnam and became a drug addict?

ANS: "Sam Stone."

46 He is known universally as, simply, Rambo. But what is this character's first name?

ANS: John.

47 What was the title of the first "Rambo" film?

ANS: *First Blood.*

48 True or false: The title of the second "Rambo" film is *Cobra.*

ANS: False.

49 What ex-professional football player has starred in a series of Vietnam fantasy films dealing with MIAs?
   a) Bubba Smith
   b) Alex Karras
   c) Dick Butkus
   d) Jimmy Brown
   e) Chuck Norris

ANS: e.

50 One song on this 1966 record by Barry Sadler was called "Letter from Vietnam." The flip side was a big hit. What was its name?

ANS: "The Ballad of the Green Berets."

51 Victor Lundberg croaked what 1967 "talking ballad" about the draft?

ANS: "An Open Letter to My Teen-Age Son."

52 What former Army helicopter pilot first became a pop star by writing "Me and Bobby McGee" and later moved big into films?

ANS: Kris Kristofferson.

53 What is the title of Lucian Truscott's novel, later made into a 1985 TV movie, about a homosexual murder at West Point during the Vietnam years?

ANS: *Dress Gray.*

54 What television station produced the PBS series *Vietnam: A Television History?*

ANS: WGBH, Boston.

55 The Boston Publishing Company was formed to produce another massive fifteen-volume series on the war and its origin. What was it called?

ANS: *The Vietnam Experience.*

56 The editor in chief of that series was assistant secretary of state for public affairs in the Kennedy and Johnson administrations before becoming editor of *The Atlantic.* He was

ANS: Robert Manning.

57 Jan Barry and William Ehrhart are two Vietnam veterans who collaborated on critically acclaimed works for *The East River Anthology*. What was this anthology?

ANS: Volumes of poetry.

58 What *New Yorker* writer wrote two moving accounts of the ground war in Vietnam, "The Village of Ben Suc" and "The Military Half"?

ANS: Jonathan Schell.

59 He was considered by many to be the leading U.S. government expert on the Vietnamese Communists. His 1966 book popularized their shortened name for American readers? What was the title? Who is the author?

ANS: *Vietcong* by Douglas Pike.

60 This Vietnam combat veteran started *Texas Monthly* magazine and swiftly rose through the ranks of journalism to become the youngest-ever editor-in-chief of *Newsweek*. He was replaced after a stormy two years and later returned to Vietnam to write his memoir. His name?

ANS: William Broyles, Jr.

61 One's father was a famous *New York Times* Washington columnist; the other's was among this country's most revered authors, writing *The Grapes of Wrath*, among other books. Both sons went to Vietnam to find literary fame and fortune and produced books about it. Like their fathers, their names are James and John. Who are they?

ANS: James Reston, Jr., and John Steinbeck IV.

62 Don Oberdorfer, then of the Knight-Ridder news service, and Peter Braestrup of *The Washington Post* both wrote highly praised books about the same 1968 cataclysmic Vietnam event. What was it?

ANS: The Tet surprise attack. Oberdorfer's book used the event as its simple title; Braestrup's was a critical study of the press performance, *Big Story.*

63 Who wrote this 1976 defense of Vietnam service, *Twenty Days and Twenty Years*—Nguyen Cao Ky or William Westmoreland?

ANS: Ky.

64 *Year Zero* was the title of this first book about Communist Cambodia by Catholic priest Francois Ponchaud. To what did it refer?

ANS: The year the Khmer Rouge under Pol Pot began rule.

65 *Decent Interval*, a 1977 book by former CIA analyst Frank Snepp, exposed CIA misdeeds at the end of the war. What did the mocking title refer to?

ANS: The claim by Henry Kissinger that Washington would give the Saigon government a "decent interval" to prepare for the U.S. departure.

66 Who wrote *Honorable Men: My Life in the CIA?*

ANS: William Colby.

67 What Hanoi general wrote the 1967 book *Big Victory, Big Task?*

   a) **Vo Nguyen Giap**
   b) **Nguyen Cao Ky**
   c) **Le Duc Tho**
   d) **Van Tien Dung**

ANS: a.

68 Who is Doris Kearns, and what did she have to do with Vietnam?

ANS: She was a close associate of LBJ and induced him to divulge facts about Vietnam that he had kept hitherto secret. They were later revealed in her 1976 book, *Lyndon Johnson and the American Dream.*

69 Who wrote the only first-person account of an American working with Ho Chi Minh during World War II?

ANS: Archimedes L. Patti, in *Why Vietnam? A Prelude to America's Albatross.*

70 True or false: The Rolling Stones supplied the opening ballad for a hit antiwar movie.

ANS: True. "Out of Time," from *Coming Home,* about a paralyzed Vietnam veteran.

71 What Vietnam-oriented film won Jon Voight and Jane Fonda Oscars for best actor and actress in 1978?

ANS: *Coming Home.*

72 Who played the disillusioned, impotent Vietnam veteran in the 1984 film *The Big Chill?*

ANS: William Hurt.

Match these authors with their books about Vietnam veterans:

73 Gloria Emerson	a)	*Bloods*
74 Myra MacPherson	b)	*Payback*
75 Wallace Terry	c)	*Winners and Losers*
76 Joe Klein	d)	*Long Time Passing*
77 Al Santoli	e)	*Everything We Had*

ANS: 73-c, 74-d, 75-a, 76-b, 77-e.

78 Name the first feature film about Vietnam, directed by and starring John Wayne.

ANS: *The Green Berets.*

79 Former infantryman Tim O'Brien wrote this National Book Award–winning novel in 1975.

ANS: *Going After Cacciato.*

80 What violent 1978 movie was about three Pennsylvania steel-mining town boys going off to Vietnam?

ANS: *The Deer Hunter.*

81 Who were the three male stars of *The Deer Hunter?*

ANS: Robert DeNiro, Christopher Walken, and John Savage.

82 Who were the two male stars, the hunter and the hunted, of *Apocalypse Now?*

ANS: Martin Sheen and Marlon Brando.

83 Which former Hollywood starlet played a serious role as Nick Nolte's girl friend in *Who'll Stop the Rain?*

ANS: Tuesday Weld.

84 *Who'll Stop the Rain* was based on an award-winning novel, *Dog Soldiers.* Who wrote it?

ANS: Robert Stone.

85 True or false: *Friendly Fire,* a popular nonfiction book by C.D.B. Bryan, was made into a TV movie starring Carol Burnett.

ANS: True.

86 What actor and actress starred in what 1977 feature film about the sad homecomings of Vietnam veterans?

ANS: Henry Winkler and Sally Field, in *Heroes.*

87 Paul Schrader, who wrote *Taxi Driver,* also wrote which of the following Vietnam films:
   a) *Rolling Thunder*
   b) *Heroes*
   c) *The Deer Hunter*

ANS: a.

88 What was surprising about the final scene of *The Deer Hunter?*
   a) the veterans wept
   b) the veterans went to see a movie about Vietnam
   c) the veterans sang "America the Beautiful"
   d) the veterans sang "God Bless America"

ANS: d.

89 This member of the Mamas and the Papas wrote "San Francisco (Be Sure and Wear Some Flowers in Your Hair)."

ANS: John Phillips.

90 As the title of the song by Mick Jagger and Keith Richard had it, when you were in Vietnam, you were how many "light years from home"?

ANS: 2,000.

91 This harmonic hard rocker from The Animals was a favorite anthem of GIs in when they wanted to get out of Vietnam.

ANS: "We Gotta Get Out of This Place (if it's the last thing we ever do)."

92 Complete these titles of works about the war in Southeast Asia:
Fields of ———, by James Webb
The ——— *Fields*, by Sydney Schanberg

ANS: *Fire; Killing.*

93 *The Killing Fields* took place in what country, in what year?

ANS: In Cambodia in 1975.

94 True or false: According to the title of an influential 1979 book by British journalist William Shawcross, Laos was a *Sideshow* to the war in Vietnam.

ANS: False. Cambodia was the sideshow.

95 Of many Western correspondents either killed or missing in Cambodia, which one was the son of an infamous swashbuckling Hollywood star of the 1940s and 1950s?
a) Julian Lennon
b) Douglas Fairbanks, Jr.
c) Sean Flynn

ANS: c.

96 What U.S. correspondent for *The St. Louis Post-Dispatch* was captured by the Khmer Rouge in 1970 but lived to write about it in *Forty Days with the Enemy?*
a) Homer Bigart
b) David Halberstam
c) Richard Dudman
d) Philip Caputo
e) Michael Herr

ANS: c.

97 *Vietnam: A History* was a book made into a thirteen-part PBS series. What journalist wrote it?

ANS: Stanley Karnow.

98 What onetime commander of all U.S. forces in Vietnam published his 1976 memoir on the war, called *A Soldier Reports?*

ANS: Gen. William Westmoreland.

99 Probably the first filmed report from Vietnam was by what U.S. television correspondent, who later became famous? It showed U.S. troops burning down a peasant's hut.

ANS: Morely Safer.

Match these three American television correspondents, who reported extensively on the war from Vietnam, with their networks:

100 Garrick Utley   a) ABC
101 Murray Fromson   b) NBC
102 Malcolm Browne   c) CBS

ANS: 100-b, 101-c, 102-a.

103 What was the term adopted by U.S. "pacification" strategists in Vietnam that later became the title of a highly critical —and critically acclaimed—documentary about the war?

ANS: *Hearts and Minds.*

104 What *New York Times* correspondent was awarded a Bronze Star for valor by the Army when he rescued a wounded Marine during the battle of Hue in 1968?
  a) Charles Mohr
  b) David Halberstam
  c) Fox Butterfield

ANS: a.

105 What was the title of the award-winning 1972 book by Frances Fitzgerald?

ANS: *Fire in the Lake.*

106 Bernard Fall's famous, landmark early book on the war was named after the nickname of what notoriously dangerous stretch of road in South Vietnam?
  a) Tu Do Street

b) Street Without Joy
c) Ho Chi Minh Trail
d) Route One
e) The Thin Red Line

ANS: b.

107 What Australian reporter covered the war from "the other," i.e., the Communist side?

ANS: Wilfred Burchett.

FACT

Very few Western reporters were able or were trusted enough to cover the war from the Communist side for any length of time. Wilfred Burchett, a tall, gray-haired Australian often covered combat from the Vietcong side. He went so far as to crawl through Communist tunnels right under Saigon troops. The author of dozens of books about these and other Communist-side adventures, Burchett was introduced to President Richard Nixon by Chinese leader Chou En-lai at a banquet in Peking in 1972. "Ah, yes," said Nixon. "You're the Australian correspondent. I've heard of you."

108 Who wrote *Soul on Ice?*
a) Bobby Seale
b) George Jackson
c) Eldridge Cleaver

ANS: c.

Match these famous anthems of their day with their authors:
109 "Where Have All the Flowers Gone?"
110 "Draft Dodger Rag"

111 "The Times They Are A-Changin' "
 a) Bob Dylan
 b) Pete Seeger
 c) Phil Ochs

ANS: 109-b, 110-c, 111-a.

112 Phil Ochs wrote and sang "I Ain't Marchin' Anymore." Who was his co-author?

ANS: Bob Gibson.

113 In the famous opening scene of *Apocalypse Now,* what actor went berserk in his Saigon hotel room with what rock group's music on the soundtrack?

ANS: Martin Sheen; The Doors.

114 In *Apocalypse Now,* what then-unknown actor briefed Sheen before he went on the mission to "terminate" Marlon Brando "with extreme prejudice"?

ANS: Harrison Ford.

115 Creedence Clearwater Revival produced a song that became the title of what classic Vietnam War movie?

ANS: *Who'll Stop the Rain?*

116 Who wrote the song "Long Time Passing"?
 a) Peter, Paul and Mary
 b) Pete Seeger
 c) Gloria Emerson
 d) Bob Dylan
 e) Myra MacPherson

ANS: b.